MEN NEAR THE TOP
Filling Key Posts in the Federal Service

COMMITTEE FOR ECONOMIC DEVELOPMENT
Supplementary Paper No. 20

MEN NEAR THE TOP

FILLING KEY POSTS IN THE FEDERAL SERVICE

BY

JOHN J. CORSON

and

R. SHALE PAUL

THE JOHNS HOPKINS PRESS
BALTIMORE

139369

Library of Congress Catalog Card Number: 66–17010

Printed in the United States of America
PUBLISHED BY THE JOHNS HOPKINS PRESS

A CED Supplementary Paper

This Supplementary Paper is issued by the Committee for Improvement of Management in Government of the Committee for Economic Development in conformity with the CED Bylaws (Art. IX, Sec. 5) which authorize the publication of a manuscript as a Supplementary Paper if:

a) It is recommended for publication by the Director of CED's Improvement of Management in Government Division because in his opinion, it "constitutes an important contribution to the understanding of a problem on which research has been initiated by the Committee for Improvement of Management in Government" and,

b) It is approved for publication by a majority of an Editorial Board on the ground that it presents "an analysis which is a significant contribution to the understanding of the problem in question."

This Supplementary Paper relates to the Statement on National Policy, *Improving Executive Management in the Federal Government*, issued by the CED Research and Policy Committee in July 1964.

The members of the Editorial Board authorizing publication of this Supplementary Paper are:

It has also been read by the Improvement of Management in Government Advisory Board.

IMPROVEMENT OF MANAGEMENT IN GOVERNMENT
ADVISORY BOARD

vi

PREFACE

This book could not be more timely. It concerns some 5,000 career people in the federal government who hold important civilian posts at the so-called supergrade level, just beneath the top political appointees. Over the coming decade, to replace losses through attrition and to fill new positions that are created as the government's size and functions expand, no less than 4,000 men and women with similar qualifications and experience will be required. This poses a formidable problem indeed in management recruiting, training, and planning.

From my own experience in the federal service, I can attest that the efficiency and effectiveness of governmental operations depend heavily on these relatively few people. They are the deputies, assistant secretaries, the assistants-to, the bureau chiefs, the budget officers, the scientific directors, the chief economists in the federal departments and agencies. They have the managerial skills, the intimate knowledge of government, and the professional and scientific capabilities needed to carry on the vast programs of the government now in being and to develop new programs. They are responsible for disbursing billions of dollars, and their duties range from the management of the Military Assistance Program to the guidance of medical research in the National Institute of Health. They provide the expertise and the continuity that make the efforts of Cabinet officers and other political appointees effective and productive.

These upper-level civil servants are hard to replace. They are mature (their average age is 52) and they have had long years of service (60 per cent of them have been with the government more than 20 years). The bulk of the 5,000 came into government during two unique periods. The first was the Depression, when many talented and educated young people could not get a foothold in business or in academic life. The second was the immediate postwar period, when veterans, anxious to return quickly to civilian life, availed themselves of the preference given veterans in government hiring. These were buyer's markets. But now government must compete with industry, and with universities, too, for the bright and promising graduates who will become the outstanding administrators and the brilliant individual "performers" in science and the professions in the era ahead. It is a seller's market.

But this is only part of the challenging personnel problem facing the federal government. The environment in which government exists rapidly changes in response to the vast social, economic, and technological changes of the past few decades.

This point was underscored by a policy statement published by the Committee for Economic Development in 1964, called "Improving Executive Management in the Federal Government," in conjunction with which this book developed. The CED statement observed that the goals of government are increasingly numerous and involved. The need for specialization and for highly trained experts in new fields has increased. Each field of knowledge is constantly enlarging, and the traditional academic and scientific disciplines are cross-fertilizing with each other and with new disciplines (e.g., astrophysics). For the manager in the federal service this has meant new problems in coordination and comprehension. He has available, and has had to learn how to use, new management tools such as mathematical programming that are more sophisticated, efficient, and expensive. "Today's executive in government, as in business, science, or engineering," noted the CED statement, "needs a broader range of competence than was required in earlier times."

This escalation to a higher level of required skills and competence, coupled with the stiff competition in the marketplace

for able and experienced manpower, has brought about an
urgent need for the improvement of the government's managerial recruitment and training programs. But before this
can be achieved, there is need to know some very basic things.
What talents are required for these posts now and in the future?
What is the proper compensation? To what extent should the
government bring experienced people into high-level jobs
from the outside rather than develop them from within?
There are many more vital questions; as for example, the
degree to which managerial techniques can be transferred
from business to government. But these questions can be
answered satisfactorily only when one knows in detail just
what people do in their jobs—and of this information in government there is all too little.

It is worthwhile pausing to examine this point a little more
fully, since it sheds light on the CED's role in this area and
places *Men Near the Top* in its proper perspective.

The authors of the book start with a simple—deceptively
simple—question, "What kind of work are upper-level civil
servants engaged in?" Now, this question—What do people
do?—is a familiar one in business and industry. It was first
asked in an organized and analytical fashion eighty years ago
by Frederick W. Taylor, who is credited with having fathered
the science of management. This is a highly pragmatic science,
and to the degree that it is scientific, it has evolved principles,
and guides, from careful observation of what people do, their
behavior, and their relationships with others in their jobs.
There is a tremendous amount of such research, based on
continuous study, in business.

There is no counterpart to this body of information in
government. Excellent studies of the organization of the
federal government indeed have been made, as for example,
by the President's Committee on Administrative Management in the 1930's and by the two Hoover Commissions after
the war. However, there was no provision for carrying on these
and other studies, so that what material does exist is frag-
mentary and much of it is now out of date.

It was, in fact, this very problem—the lack of a continuing organization dedicated to the study of management in government—that led directly to the CED's involvement in this area. Four years ago, I was approached by a group of men, including officials in the Kennedy Administration and former officials of the Eisenhower Administration, who wanted to establish such a continuing body. It seemed to me that what was proposed would fit very closely to the CED's purposes and procedures. CED is a citizen group of businessmen and educators, and its charter requires it to consider policy recommendations "without regard to and independently of the special interests of any group in the body politic, either political, social, or economic." It also utilizes the best available research on any subject it may study, and it works with a distinguished group of advisors from the academic world. Furthermore, in much of CED's past and current work we have tried to define the appropriate role of government in our society, and to suggest how to get more for the money government spends.

The trustees agreed that the proposal would be a suitable one for CED to pursue, and in May, 1963, they established, as a standing committee of the parent organization, the Committee for Improvement of Management in Government (CIMG). The committee is comprised of 25 members of CED and ten members from the outside, all of whom are top businessmen with extensive lay experience. Collectively, the group has had an impressive amount of government experience, inasmuch as it includes four former cabinet secretaries, three former undersecretaries, two heads of commissions, as well as others who have held high posts in government. The committee's work, aided by a staff in Washington, is financed largely by grants from the Carnegie Corporation of New York, Rockefeller Brothers Fund, W. K. Kellogg Foundation, Edgar Stern Family Fund, Six Foundation, and others.

CIMG has undertaken a broad program of studies, and has had the satisfaction of seeing some of its early efforts bear fruit. One policy statement, "Presidential Succession and Inability," received strong editorial support, and many of its recommendations are embodied in the proposed Twenty-fifth

Amendment to the Constitution. Recommendations made in "Improving Executive Management in the Federal Government" likewise have found acceptance, as in the case of the recent increase in government salaries. An office also has been established in the White House to develop a roster of executive talent for high-level appointments.

Men Near the Top, by filling some of the gaps in basic research, helps make possible further improvement in the management of the federal service. To find the answer to the question "What do people do?," the authors sent a lengthy questionnaire to a random sample of the 5,000 key people on the upper-level of the federal service. The main body of material on which this study is based was drawn from the 424 replies received, as well as from extensive personal interviewing. The respondents were asked to describe in detail all their activities during a typical week and to evaluate the comparative worth and significance of these activities. They were also asked about their educational experience and their job history in the government.

This material yields important information regarding what people *actually* do in contrast with the sterile official descriptions of job function and responsibility. It likewise offers realistic insight into the public servant's relationship with his superiors, with his colleagues, with other federal bureaus and agencies, with Congress, and with constituents and pressure groups on the outside. The authors have made a particularly valuable contribution in categorizing with great care the three different types of upper-level career jobs—program manager, supporting staff manager, professional—and in stressing the differences in the work and responsibility of each. As a result, there should be less confusion in the future about the concept of "management"—in the accepted sense of planning, organizing, and controlling—as it applies or does not apply to the federal service.

What is presented here, it is important to note, is largely the public servant's *own* view of his work, his responsibilities, and his relationships, with interpretation and analysis by the authors. This book is not—and the authors make no pretense that it is—a definitive or final answer to the important questions that they ask at the outset. But here is a noteworthy beginning; the book makes possible further analytical studies of a subject that is of great meaning to all citizens, yet about which surprisingly little is known.

MARION B. FOLSOM
Chairman, Committee for Improvement of Management in Government of the Committee for Economic Development

AUTHORS' ACKNOWLEDGMENT

A BOOK—THE IDEAS that gave birth to it, the time-consuming analyses that went into it, the laborious but often exhilarating task of writing it, and the meticulous work involved in critically reviewing, editing, and indexing—infrequently is the product solely of the individual or individuals whose names appear on the title page. And so it is with this book.

The idea that there was needed a clearer, more precise understanding of what those men and women in top-level career jobs in the federal government do, as a basis for improving the ways in which civil servants are recruited, trained, promoted, developed, and compensated, originated with John J. Corson. The analyses of the large volume of data on which this study was based were carried out under the continuing direction of R. Shale Paul. But a book eventually has to be written. The authors shared this task. Each chapter is the product of writing and rewriting by both authors.

The fulfillment of this project, however, was made possible by (a) the encouragement and assistance of key officials of the United States Civil Service Commission and (b) the generous cooperation of nearly 500 men and women in top-level federal jobs, who gave of their time to complete questionnaires on which this study was based. We trust that these individuals will find in the conclusions and recommendations presented in this book a useful reward for their generous efforts.

In addition, the authors were aided in many ways by colleagues on the staff of McKinsey & Company, who conducted many of the interviews with respondents and supplied valuable ideas. Substantial assistance in the early stage of the study was provided by Belva O'Leary MacDonald, who was granted a leave by the United States Civil Service Commission to permit her to participate in the early efforts that went into this book. Joanne Stephenson Hayes and Vera Ullrich worked tirelessly over a long period in collecting and tabulating data and in typing and retyping the manuscript.

The authors are indebted to those individuals who gave time to reviewing and criticizing successive drafts of this manuscript—Edward McCrensky of the Department of the Navy; Rufus E. Miles, Jr. of the Department of Health, Education, and Welfare; Wallace S. Sayre of Columbia University; Rocco C. Siciliano of the Pacific Maritime Association; O. Glen Stahl of the Civil Service Commission; David T. Stanley of The Brookings Institution; Paul P. Van Riper of Cornell University, and Philip E. Young of the United States Council of the International Chamber of Commerce. Their incisive reactions and criticisms were invaluable in enabling the authors to refine and improve the text.

Finally, substantial thanks are due to the Carnegie Corporation and the Committee for Economic Development. The Carnegie staff thought well of the idea and provided generous and needed financial support. The Committee for Economic Development continued this assistance by enabling Shale Paul to contribute his time and effort, by providing many miscellaneous supporting services, and by arranging for the publication of this book.

JOHN J. CORSON
R. SHALE PAUL

CONTENTS

LIST OF TABLES

Chapter I

AN INTRODUCTION TO THE TOP-LEVEL CIVIL SERVANT

THERE ARE, near the top of the hierarchy that runs this country's federal government, about 5,000 men and women whose activities vitally affect the lives of every American. With few exceptions their names are unknown to most Americans. The titles of the jobs they hold are similarly little known and the suspicion is widespread that these jobs require neither arduous effort, great talent, or imagination. Their compensation, in comparison with that of many business and professional men, leads many Americans to infer that they are less capable, that they work for government because they could not hold their own in private enterprise.

Yet this relatively small group of men and women occupy a critical place in the management of our government. If only by their location near the top of the most powerful government in the world, they can (and do) exercise considerable and increasing power.

Not in recent years has any substantial attempt been made to describe *what* they do.[1] In these years, the work of the federal

[1] Perhaps the last significant work that viewed upper-level career civil servants in terms of *what* they do was A. MacMahon and J. Millett's *Federal Administrators* (New York: Columbia University Press, 1939), which pictured the work of "bureau directors."

government has changed markedly and expanded materially. Hence, this book is designed to picture what these men and women do, how they carry out the tasks for which they are responsible, and what skills and talents are required.

This book pictures the activities and the experiences of top-level career civil servants as described by the individuals themselves. It does not presume that these activities are necessarily those that should consume the time of these individuals; nor does it imply that the educational and work experience these individuals had prior to reaching their present positions is that which best equips them for their present responsibilities. In the latter chapters (VI and VII), we present recommendations as to the recruitment and development of men and women who will occupy similar positions in the future. Stated in other words, this book, after picturing what these key officials do and their relationships to their better known political superiors, suggests answers to such questions as these:

   —How to sustain and increase the quality of this vital group in the future, i.e., to provide a reservoir of talent to fill the place of those who retire, die, or are displaced.
   —How to replenish this reservoir at the bottom with intelligent and capable young people, and at upper levels with more seasoned individuals who possess needed skills.
   —How to ensure that the successive jobs and training given the individual as he rises in the federal service equip him to carry the responsibilities he bears when he reaches the top.

The recommendations this book presents point the way for the President, his department and agency heads, the United States Civil Service Commission, and the Congress to improve the ways by which the individuals in this group are originally recruited, and subsequently developed, compensated, and motivated. To ensure that the numerous departments and agencies of the federal government have effective and responsible direction; that our national defense is impregnable; that taxes are fairly assessed and collected, the aged are provided for, our natural resources conserved, the mails delivered, and the housing conditions in our slums improved— to ensure all this and much more, nothing could be more important than to ensure the capabilities and the zeal of those 5,000 men and women who serve near the top.

Other studies have dealt with top-level federal civil servants. One describes the social, economic, and educational backgrounds of federal executives and their families.[2] Another appraises various features of a personnel system for the higher civil service and considers the attractiveness of federal careers through the eyes of present and former federal employees.[3] Still a third is concerned with the image of federal service as held by employees themselves, the business community, college and high school groups, and the public generally.[4]

This study focuses on the *functions performed* by these men and women. It strives to answer the apparently simple question, "What kinds of work are upper-level civil servants engaged in?" In short, "What do they do?" The answer to that question will reveal what influence and power they exercise and will suggest the talents and capabilities required. But first it is proposed to identify this small group more precisely and to show where they fit in the power structure of the American federal government.

WHO "RUNS" THE FEDERAL GOVERNMENT?

Numerous overly simplified answers can be, and usually are, given in response to the question: "Who runs the federal government?" If one refers to the Executive Branch, a logical

[2] *The American Federal Executive*, by W. L. Warner, P. P. Van Riper, N. H. Martin, and O. F. Collins (New Haven: Yale University Press, 1963), traces the family, social, and economic backgrounds of federal executives and describes to some extent their own education and public careers, as well as the private and public world in which they operate.

[3] *The Higher Civil Service*, by David T. Stanley (Washington, D. C.: The Brookings Institution, 1964), discusses the appeals of federal service in terms of over 500 interviews with present and past civilian career employees.

[4] *The Image of the Federal Service*, by F. P. Kilpatrick, M. C. Cummings, and M. K. Jennings (Washington, D.C.: The Brookings Institution, 1964), is a lengthy analysis, based on over 5,000 interviews, of the occupational values, appeals, and satisfactions of federal employment as seen by the federal civil servants themselves, the business community, and other major groups within the United States.

answer might be, "the President." But the President depends upon a vast bureaucracy without which he would be helpless in discharging the numerous and infinitely important tasks that make up his job.

That bureaucracy is headed by approximately 9,000 individuals who occupy the topmost posts. Collectively, these men and women can be said to "run" the Executive Branch of the federal government. Their number includes political executives, military officers, foreign service officers, and career officials—the largest single group.

Political executives are the men and women who help to convert the philosophy and aims of the winning political party into practical programs. At the very top, there are 500–750 key officials, appointed by the President to reflect his views and policies in the conduct of each agency, board, and department. These include Cabinet members and their Under Secretaries and Assistant Secretaries, agency heads and their deputies, and the members of boards, commissions, and regulatory agencies.

Beneath these presidential appointees at the top are those political positions at lower levels—about 700—that are made by the appointees themselves as they assume control of their respective organizations.

Both those appointed by the President (such as the Secretary of Interior) and those appointed by the presidential appointees to top-level positions (such as the Director of the National Park Service) are regarded as policy-makers and as overseers of the way in which policy is carried out. In practice however, the roles of each involve substantial management responsibilities and, hence, require a thorough knowledge of substantive agency programs. Typically, many of these appointees are brought in at the change of an administration or at a new presidential term, hopefully to serve for its duration. But the stay of many political executives is short (perhaps thirty to thirty-six months in the government, less in a single position), and the task of political recruiting a continuing one.

Military officers, nearly 1,300 of flag rank, play a major part in formulating the policies, planning the expenditures, and directing about two-thirds of all individuals employed in the Executive Branch of the federal government. Of the nearly 3.8 million people employed by the Department of Defense, well over one-fourth are civilian employees. The direction of both military and civilian manpower in the performance and support of many functions required to operate and maintain adequate national defense is carried out by military officers. They execute day-to-day assignments quite similar to those performed by career officials in positions at upper levels of the civilian career service.

Foreign Service officers, again about 1,300 of them, include members of the Foreign Service, the Foreign Service Reserve (at grades FSO 1 and FSO 2 or their equivalents), and career ambassadors and ministers. They serve in foreign affairs agencies (State Department, Agency for International Development [AID] and United States Information Agency [USIA]), in the United States and in diplomatic posts abroad, and are responsible for the conduct of consular, economic, political, and administrative operations in more than 100 foreign countries.

Top career civilians make up most of the federal top management group. At levels just below the political appointees in the federal hierarchy, are the 5,000 men and women in the top three echelons of the classified civil service (the "supergrades," General Schedule-16, GS-17, and GS-18) and the Postal Field Service (grades 18, 19, and 20), and in positions provided for under Public Law 313[5] and similar statutes. This group includes, in addition, individuals who serve in similar managerial or professional positions in the Atomic Energy Commission (AEC), the Tennessee Valley Authority (TVA), the United States Public Health Service, the Veterans Administration's Department of Medicine and Surgery, and other agencies outside of the competitive civil service.

These 5,000 men and women are responsible for implementing the policies established by their political superiors. In

---

[5] These "PL 313" positions were established to facilitate recruitment of individuals with special scientific or technical skills by a limited number of federal agencies. See Appendix A for a description of federal grades and pay scales.

practice, they play a significant role in formulating governmental policies, for they provide the long experience, the intimate knowledge, and often the essential insight on which politically appointed executives must rely in order to discharge effectively their policymaking and overseeing responsibilities.

A LOOK AT THREE TOP CAREER CIVILIANS

A more life-like introduction to those at the top of the federal career service can be provided by means of brief sketches of three upper-level officials who are currently working "near the top." Each does a different kind of work in a separate federal agency, but all illustrate the responsible and rewarding work being done by men and women who serve at the upper levels of the career federal service.

Manlio F. De Angelis, number-three man in the Bureau of African Affairs, AID, is Deputy Administrator for Management. A veteran of twenty-five years of federal service, Mr. De Angelis is concerned with the effectiveness of the operations and with the costs of AID's loan and technical assistance programs in thirty-four African nations. These programs, incidentally, involve the expenditure of more than $200 million annually. Among other things, Mr. De Angelis has worked to forward a project to consolidate the administrative services and support functions in six of the African countries so as to serve simultaneously all United States agencies operating in a given country. In early 1964 he was assigned to set up a regional United States AID Mission in Washington to serve thirteen African nations. He exercised the authority of a mission director and set up an appropriate staff to provide both program and management support for the AID programs in these countries. Mounting such an effort from Washington may sound absurd until one considers that it is often necessary to place a telephone call through Paris or London to talk from one African nation—say, an ex-French colony—to another African nation—say, a British colony.

Mr. De Angelis brought to his job in AID experience in several agencies—the Civil Service Commission, the Bureau of the Budget, the Department of Health, Education, and Welfare (HEW), and the Economic Cooperation Administration. For these federal agencies, he has served in Japan and Greece, and has traveled extensively in Africa. In addition, he took a two-year leave of absence to teach graduate-level public administration at the University of Bologna, Italy (1958–60).

William M. Leffingwell, Deputy Director of Military Assistance in the Office of the Assistant Secretary of Defense for International Security Affairs, is the highest ranking civil servant primarily and directly concerned with the management of a program "to promote the peace of the world and the foreign policy, security, and general welfare of the United States." Guided by that congressional statement of policy and the related implementing provisions in the Foreign Assistance Act, Mr. Leffingwell works with and, in his absence, acts for the Director of Military Assistance—a four star general—in administering the multinational, multibillion-dollar program known as Military Assistance through which the United States participates in and helps to support free world collective security.

Managing the Military Assistance Program is an extremely complex undertaking because it involves the provision of a wide variety of military equipment—tanks, guns, ships, aircraft, and all the related items that go to equip a military force—to the armed forces of more than fifty allied and friendly nations which share with the United States both the benefits and the burdens of common defense against aggressive international communism. It also involves decisions which cannot be taken unilaterally within the Department of Defense, but require continuous close coordination of plans and programs with other elements of the government, such as the Department of State, AID, the Bureau of the Budget, and the Treasury Department. One of Mr. Leffingwell's primary responsibilities is to participate in the decision-making process through which courses of action are developed with a view to promoting the predominant national interest in any given situation, and to ensure that the resultant military assistance plans and programs are so designed as to make the maximum possible contribution to the attainment of agreed, established, and specific objectives—political, economic, and military.

Because attainment of these objectives depends also on the availability of funds appropriated by the Congress, another of Mr. Leffingwell's major responsibilities is that of supervising and participating in the annual presentation to the Congress of the Administration's budget request for support of the Military Assistance Program. Four congressional committees hold extended hearings each year before reporting to the House and Senate their recommendations with respect to legislation and appropriations for military assistance. Voluminous narrative and statistical justification for proposed world-wide military assistance programs are prepared to support the testimony of the Secretaries of State and Defense, the Chairman of the Joint Chiefs of Staff, and other Executive Branch witnesses. For many years, Mr. Leffingwell has been the key official in the Department of Defense responsible for ensuring adequate preparation for the effective, convincing, and successful presentation to the Congress of the Administration's annual request for military assistance authorization and appropriations.

The use to which funds granted by Congress are put is, of course, Mr. Leffingwell's paramount concern in the day-to-day operation of the Office of the Director of Military Assistance. His office is a major factor in preventing waste or mismanagement. He may be "on the carpet" when a visiting monarch from the Middle East complains that the American bulldozers he received don't work. Though such instances are of an isolated nature, they often make headlines and serve to prejudice public opinion against the entire program.

What experience does Mr. Leffingwell bring to these tasks? He began as a junior Army officer in 1917, spent over twenty years between wars in private business, and rejoined the Army in World War II. Later, in Washington, he was assigned to the Lend-Lease program. Here, his interest and experience in the tasks relating to the provision of people, goods, and dollars to other countries began. He thus has more than twenty years of experience in problems of providing assistance to needy nations abroad and has helped to direct the expenditure of more than $33 billion into those channels most likely to enhance the security of the United States by strengthening the self- and common-defense capabilities of its free world friends and allies.

Ellen Winston runs the Welfare Administration in the United States Department of Health, Education, and Welfare. As Commissioner of Welfare, she—more perhaps than any other one person in the country—can and is expected to influence the nation's welfare programs and policies. Specifically, she has a major voice in federal policy relating to state-federal programs which involve:

—the expenditure of more than $5 billion for the maintenance of, and services to, dependent persons;

—the efficiency and effectiveness of fifty state welfare departments, and the large city and other local welfare departments through which most of these funds are expended; and

—the well-being of more than eight million recipients of public assistance and many other persons receiving a growing range of welfare services.

Her role and responsibilities are likely to grow. The enactment of Medicare is a single illustration of the trend toward persistent expansion of government's social welfare activities.

How does the Commissioner discharge these sizable and growing responsibilities? To begin with, she directs the efforts of a 1200-member staff. This she does through weekly meetings with her administrative staff, daily sessions with the Deputy Commissioner and other key individuals, small group meetings with top staff members, and other meetings with the operating heads and staffs of major organizational units of the Welfare Administration. But running the shop involves more than simply holding meetings; it means phone calls, dictation, and the personal review and reading of selected mail, staff papers, and technical reports.

Even more important to the success of the program are Mrs. Winston's responsibilities *outside* the Welfare Administration itself. For "managing the program" involves as well: meetings with the Secretary of Health, Education, and Welfare and the Assistant Secretary for Legislation as part of her continual efforts to formulate and adjust changing and newly developing programs; sessions with representatives of as many as a dozen other federal agencies that administer pieces of the welfare program; meetings on the Hill to speak for her programs and to testify as to the money needed to carry them out; and numerous contacts with state welfare agencies and associations. And in a program so interrelated with state and local governments, Mrs. Winston cannot escape (and doesn't attempt to) the inevitable burden—borne by many public servants—of carrying her program to the public. She speaks regularly before large national, regional, and state meetings (e.g., the National Conference on Social Welfare), attends other meetings and conferences (on aging, day care, and so forth), and entertains individuals who come in from all over the United States and abroad to talk about the program.

Mrs. Winston's qualifications for both the internal "management" and external "leadership" aspects of her job include M.A. and Ph.D. degrees in sociology and more than thirty years of relevant experience. She began federal service in 1934 as a social economist with the Works Progress Administration. In succeeding years, she served with the Farm Security Administration and the National Resources Planning Board, and served as Commissioner of Public Welfare in North Carolina. Between times, she taught and headed up the Sociology Department of Meredith College and lectured as a visiting professor at the University of North Carolina.

These brief descriptions illustrate the variety and importance of work done by those near the top. They provide, however, but a partial exposure to the real work that goes on in these top posts. To show more fully what these key people do, is the purpose of this book.

GAINS FROM BETTER UNDERSTANDING
OF THE CAREER CIVILIAN'S ROLE

What is to be gained from knowing more about *what* top career civilians do with their time? Why should a citizen—a taxpayer, a scholar, or a businessman—understand what those at the top of the career service do? There are at least three reasons why *what* they do is even more significant than *who* they are or *where* they came from.

1. *The Basis for Essential Decisions.* Only on the basis of a clear understanding of what top-career officials do—what activities consume their time, what responsibilities they bear, and hence what talents are required—can good decisions be made as to the kinds of people to be recruited, the successive types of work experience they need, the training and education that should supplement this experience, and the levels of pay that will equitably compensate those who perform these tasks. Such decisions have been founded largely on the *responsibilities assigned* rather than on a realistic analysis of what career civil servants do in carrying out these responsibilities.[6] The insights that can be gained from a concrete knowledge of the work done at upper-career levels can provide a better basis for making these decisions in the future.

2. *An Improved Understanding of Public Management.* A second gain from such an analysis may be of special benefit to the student of public administration. It is to give more precise meaning to the concept of "management" as it obtains in the Executive Branch of the government.

The utility of this much-used term, management, is diminished by the looseness with which it is often applied. Illustrations can be found of its use to describe (a) the activities of a supervisor of a group of twenty clerks and the activities of the Commissioner of Internal Revenue Service who is responsible for the work of 60,000 employees, (b) the activities of a bureau chief responsible for the accomplishments of the whole bureau

---

[6] See for confirming analysis, "The Job(s) of Management," by T. A. Mahoney, T. H. Jerdee, and S. J. Carroll, *Industrial Relations* (Institute of Industrial Relations, University of California at Berkeley), Vol. 4, No. 2, February, 1965.

and those of a division chief who carries out the established plans within a limited segment of the bureau's operations, and (c) the activities of the personnel officer (the "assistant to" the bureau chief) as well as those of the political appointee to whom the bureau chief reports.

Management, the conventional wisdom would have us believe, involves a series of interrelated processes wherever it is carried on; i.e., in a business enterprise, a government bureau, a university, or even a military unit. These processes—planning, organizing, directing, controlling, evaluating, and appraising—comprise the management job whether it involves the direction of a scientific laboratory, a staff of lawyers enforcing antitrust laws, a large post office, or a private or governmental shipyard.[7] And conventional wisdom suggests that the individual who is skilled in these processes, whether his experience be in a field of government activity wholly unrelated, or in a private business enterprise, can effectively manage any particular government program.

What indeed does the term "manage" mean? And more important, what—if anything—is distinctive about management as it is practiced in the federal service?

3. *Greater Prestige for the Public Servant.* Much also will be gained if citizens have a better understanding of the nature of the tasks performed by those in responsible career positions. That gain will be measured in the higher regard that citizens hold for the federal service as a profession. The recent Kilpatrick study[8] noted that many in the business community, in college graduating classes, and in the public generally consider working for the federal government as more secure, more routine and monotonous, and less challenging than in private industry. Yet, the same study points out that many have little real understanding of the kinds of work involved at responsible levels in federal service; many respondents characterized their idea of a typical public servant as a postman or a tax collector. And the study significantly pointed

---

[7] "Notes on a General Theory of Administration," by Edward H. Litchfield, *Administrative Science Quarterly*, Vol. I, No. 1, June, 1956, pp. 3–29.

[8] Kilpatrick, *et al., op. cit.*

out that many citizens do not think of public servants as "managers" or "executives."

> In the general public . . . 38 per cent mention this kind of work (management) as characteristic of business and only 14 per cent connect it with government. And in every other non-federal group, the business world has a long lead over the government in the extent to which it is identified with these highly prestigious activities. For example, half or more of the college seniors and graduate students mention management activities in business, but only one in five do so for government.[9]

The fact is that those at or near the top of the career service have highly responsible jobs in terms of the number of employees directed, the dollars expended, and the facilities employed. Their responsibilities are of great consequence to the well-being of citizens; in major part, they plan and carry out the government's efforts to develop and utilize atomic energy, to reduce unemployment, to curb inflation, to explore outer space, and to discover the causes and cures of cancer, heart disease, and mental illness. Throughout more than eighty federal departments and agencies, a host of virtually unknown career men and women daily direct the work of thousands of employees, spend millions, and make decisions of a scope and complexity exceeding or comparable to those made by executives of the largest private enterprise.

NATURE OF THE ANALYSIS

This study is based on a random sampling of those who served in early 1963, in civil service positions classified in grades GS-16, -17, and -18 and in positions provided for under Public Law 313. The sample was designed with the aid of statisticians from the United States Civil Service Commission; the selection of 817 individuals to whom questionnaires were mailed was made by the Commission's staff. Efforts were made—by mail and phone, and through the personnel directors in a number of agencies—to encourage recipients to complete the questionnaires. In all, a total of

[9] *Ibid.*, p. 237.

443 replies was received, of which 19 were rejected because of insufficient data. Analysis of the replies indicated that the 424 usable replies were substantially proportionate to the questionnaires mailed out in terms of representativeness by agency, by occupational categories, and by grade of position occupied.

Each of 424 individuals submitting usable replies completed a detailed questionnaire designed to reveal: (a) the nature of all activities that consumed his time for a typical week, (b) the individual's judgment as to which of these activities to which he devoted his time were "most significant" and which were "least significant," (c) a summary of the individual's education, and (d) a step-by-step analysis of the individual's work experience since his entry into the federal service.[10] The latter data as to work experience not only reveal how he reached his present post and suggest the skills and experience which he brought to it, but provide a basis for speculating as to the adequacy of the experience he gained while on the way up, to enable him to cope with the responsibilities he now bears.[11]

[10] A somewhat oversimplified picture of the "typical" supergrade emerges from the data collected in this study. This statistical profile should not be construed to imply that *all* upper level civil servants fit a single mould (actual percentages of the survey sample are shown in parentheses), for they do not! With this reservation then, the "typical" supergrade is: male (99 per cent); married (96 per cent); fifty-two years old (numerical average); a college graduate with an advanced degree (60.1 per cent). He began federal service in 1945 or earlier (69 per cent) at grade GS-7 or below (54.7 per cent). And he has worked, since his entry into federal service, in only one (39.2 per cent) or two (27.4 per cent) bureaus throughout his entire federal career. And in many cases (47.4 per cent of the respondents) he is still in the same agency in which he began his career.

More complete summarizations of the data developed in this study are included as Appendix B at the back of this book.

[11] A copy of the questionnaire used in this analysis is included as Appendix C. The techniques reflected by that questionnaire and its usage are adapted from those employed by S. Carlson in his *Executive Behavior* (Stockholm: Strombergs, 1951); by M. M. Mandell and S. H. Greenberg in their descriptive study of 50 career officials, *Major Factors in the Job of a Federal Executive* (an internal report of the Personnel Measurement Research and Development Center of the United States Civil Service Commission, July, 1962); and by W. O. Underwood in " A Hospital Director's Administrative Profile," an unpublished study made in 1959. The results of Underwood's study were subsequently published in *Hospital Administration*, Vol. 8, No. 4, Fall, 1963.

From among this randomly selected group of individuals asked to complete questionnaires, some eighty individuals, selected at random to provide a representative sub-sample of the larger group, participated in extended face-to-face interviews. The purpose of these interviews was to:

—ensure a full understanding of the responses included in the questionnaire;

—explore the part which the individual plays in the processes of decision-making in his agency;

—examine the relationships involved in the performance of each individual's job, i.e., the relative amounts of time spent with his boss, his subordinates, respresentatives of other bureaus or offices in the department, representatives of other departments, members of Congress, individuals from outside the government, and others;

—ascertain the satisfaction these respondents derive from their jobs and the dissatisfaction they suffer;

—obtain the opinions of the respondents as to the extent of their dependence in their particular jobs on (a) the knowledge of the substantive field in which each works; e.g., labor law legislation, food and drug legislation; or (b) the understanding of the process of administration.

The results of these analyses and the meaning of these interviews are interpreted, in subsequent chapters, in the light of an aggregate of the authors' forty years of experience in the federal service or as observers of its operations. The reader is forewarned that the views subsequently expressed reflect the authors' opinions, and indeed could not be a sheer recitation of statistics derived from questionnaires and interviews.

CATEGORIZING CAREER CIVILIANS AT THE TOP

Analyses of the activities of these men and women who have reached the topmost levels of the federal service, and the subsequent interviews with a portion of the total, picture effectively the careers that brought them to their present positions, the activities that now consume their time, and the roles they perform, and provide a wealth of detail reflecting the nature of their individual jobs. The data collected and the reports of these interviews, moreover, make it apparent that a wide variety of skills and talents are required of career civilians in positions at upper levels of the Executive Branch. The aggregate of these positions require men competent in many skills. These skills range from accounting and biology to weather forecasting and zoology. Further, they require of the individuals possessing such skills different kinds of talents— administrative, advisory, entrepreneurial, negotiatory, program formulation, public relations, and others—in various combinations. How then can one categorize these upper-level positions to lead to meaningful conclusions?

Other studies have categorized all positions at these levels of the federal service as "executive" positions.[12] Yet analysis makes clear that these positions are not all "executive" in character, if by that term is meant a position requiring the incumbent to plan and direct the work of other individuals to accomplish the over-all objectives of an organization.

Traditionally, positions at the upper levels of large organizations, both private and public, have been categorized as "line" or "staff." Yet analyses of the positions occupied by individuals in this study make manifest that these traditional categories do not fit well the roles of the "general counsel," the "personnel director," the "chief economist," the "budget officer," or the "scientific director" in the Executive Branch. For the occupants of such positions have hierarchal allegiances and degrees of independence that belie the traditional definition of the *staff* officer as "an extension" of the executive, i.e., of the *line* officer. And "bureau chiefs" and "division chiefs" can not aptly be categorized as "line" officers, for in their relationships with others they lack authority and status customarily associated with the line officer in the military or in private enterprise.

The analyses made in this study suggest that the more than 5,000 men and women at the top of the federal career service can usefully be divided into three groups:[13]

[12] P. T. David and R. Pollock, *Executives for Government* (Washington, D.C.: The Brookings Institution, 1957); and Warner, *et al., op. cit.*

[13] The proportions in each group have been compared with available manpower data from other services (i.e., Department of State and Department of Defense, and Atomic Energy Commission), and found to be generally consistent with the assignments of individuals serving in analogus echelons in those agencies.

Program Managers. Perhaps 35 per cent of the 5,000 serve as bureau chiefs, office heads, and division directors, and are responsible for accomplishing a "program" (or a distinguishable segment of a program) of direct service to the public. For example, the Director of the Division of Timber Management in the United States Forest Service plans and directs the sale of one-fifth of the nation's supply of timber. He is responsible each year for the accomplishment of a substantial federal program (government sales totaled $135 million in 1963) that involves the planning and direction of the activities of thousands of employees engaged in maintaining, developing, and marketing the supplies of timber on the public lands controlled by the Forest Service.

Supporting Staff Managers. Another 35 per cent provide essential administrative and personal support to the presidential appointees or to career executives who serve as program managers. These individuals function either as purveyors of managerial services (budget and fiscal, personnel, management analysis, general administration) or as deputies or assistants-to. In the National Aeronautics and Space Administration (NASA), for example, the Chief of the Management Analysis Division heads up a small shop (fifteen men) that has been instrumental in helping the administrator to hammer out the policies, procedures, and operating changes needed to accomplish NASA's third reorganization in five years. The stakes are not small; NASA's budget last year totaled nearly $5 billion.

The deputies, or assistants-to, make up less than one-third of this category, yet many serve close to the top political or career administrator and exert considerable influence over agency policies and programs. For example, the Assistant for Logistics in the Air Force who advises and consults on policies and procedures involving logistical support works directly for the Air Force Deputy Chief of Staff for Systems and Logistics.

Professionals. Almost 30 per cent of all upper-level civil servants are engaged in the practice of a profession. They serve as lawyers, economists, actuaries, directors of scientific laboratories, or as advisors in other professional fields. They are usually supported by staffs, often small, who are members of the same profession or sometimes of allied professions. A minority of the professionals perform scientific or technical tasks *alone* with little or no supporting staff to assist them. One such "performer," for example, is the Special Assistant for Fisheries and Wildlife in the Department of State. A marine biologist and international fisheries expert, he assists in developing all United States fishery policies and acts as a principal contact between fishing industry interests and the Department.

These three categories—*program managers, supporting staff managers,* and *professionals*—provide a framework for examining the differences in roles among upper-level career civil servants in the federal government. They represent—in the authors' judgment—distinctive differences in work, responsibilities, and career patterns among those so grouped. The categories themselves resulted from an analysis of the individual positions as they were perceived and described by the respondents. They do not reflect the tremendous variety and sometimes critical importance of the jobs performed by the individuals themselves. And each of the categories inevitably includes individuals who, at earlier stages in their careers, would have been classified in one of the other categories. But the categories do provide a basis for understanding the federal government's need for capable people to manage large programs, and to supply the essential, specialized technical and administrative support needed to translate programs, policies, and objectives into services for citizens.

The purpose of the next three chapters (II, III, and IV) is to show the functions for which each of these three separate groups of career servants is responsible. These chapters provide a factual picture of the activities of these people and of the ways in which they spend their time.

Those who contemplate a career in the federal civil service will learn from these chapters that the three separate groupings offer quite different career opportunities. These opportunities, in turn, demand different attitudes and interests and varied kinds of especial competence.

Chapter V describes the routes that lead to top-level positions. It suggests the kinds and breadth of experience gained as people rise over a period of approximately twenty years to top level positions in the career service. It points out the extent to which individuals move from one type of position to another (from program manager, say, to supporting staff manager). And it indicates, for those who contemplate careers in the federal service, the extent to which each type of position constitutes a separate career line.

Finally, Chapters VI and VII discuss the implications of the finding of this study. They present recommendations for changes in existing recruitment, compensation, assignment, promotion, and development practices that now determine the caliber of individuals in these top-level positions.

Chapter II

THE PROGRAM MANAGER—
A REAL-LIFE PICTURE

JOHN WASON IS IN the travel business. With a fifty-eight-member staff and an annual budget of nearly $2.5 million, he sells Europeans, Asians, Latin Americans, and others travel to the United States. Judging by the statistics, he is doing rather well; in the three years 1961–64, travel to the United States has increased by 86 per cent.

Success in the travel business requires diligent and continuous effort. Mr. Wason continually studies what attracts foreign travelers to this country, in an effort to improve selling activities in his nine overseas offices and the forty-six countries where he and his staff are involved. He has underway marketing research studies in some fifteen major areas of the world including the United Kingdom, Japan, Mexico, and Australia. But he must know his own country as well; he routinely maintains an up-to-date store of travel information on each of the fifty states.

As a travel advocate, Mr. Wason finds himself on the road a good deal of the time. In the last nine months, he has made two trips around Europe and one to Australia, and he has made speeches in a dozen cities across the United States. His regular acquaintances on these trips include (aside from his own staff members abroad) New York advertising executives, principals in airline and shipping companies and associations, hotel corporations, foreign and American travel writers, and a host of state and federal officials throughout the United States.

Many of his activities are similar to those of business executives who earn their living by promoting travel. But John Wason is hardly a typical travel executive. For he is a federal employee (grade GS-16, $18,935–$24,175). As Director of Travel Promotion, he is responsible to the Director of the United States Travel Service (who is a presidential appointee). This agency of the Department of Commerce has spearheaded efforts to bring visitors to the United States from abroad. Unlike his counterparts in airline and shipping firms who sell travel on *their* planes or ships to the many destinations served by *their* companies, Mr. Wason promotes travel to a single destination (the United States) by any means of getting there. And as a federal employee his success is not measured by "profits." He is judged, by his superiors, by the Congress, and by those for whom foreign travelers mean business, on the more numerous and much less precise grounds of how well he serves their special interests.

Approximately 1,300 individuals serve in upper levels of the civil service of this country's federal government in positions in which they, like Mr. Wason, are responsible for carrying out all or part of a formally established program. They comprise about 35 per cent of those at the upper levels of the federal career service. A very general profile of these individuals and their experience is presented in Table 1.

The programs for which they are responsible range from such conventional governmental activities as the collection of taxes, the delivery of mail, and the enforcement of antitrust laws, to programs for marketing one-fifth of all timber sold in the United States, managing the largest civilian aerial photography business in the country, and maintaining and operating a fleet of civilian aircraft that includes more planes than are operated by one of the major trunk airlines. In other words, there are upper-level civil servants responsible for carrying out each of the foregoing programs; that is, for direct-

Table 1. A Profile of the Program Manager Compared with
all Upper-Level Civil Servants*

	Program Manager	All Upper-Level Civil Servants
Average age	53.6	52.0
Marital status	94% Married	96% Married
Education: *Per cent* of college graduates with at least one advanced degree	57.1	60.1
Field of study: *Per cent* listing law, economics, or engineering	45.6	43.6
Entry into federal service: *Per cent* entering prior to 1940	63.9	50.9
Length of federal service: *Per cent* with more than twenty years	67.3	59.9
Starting grade: *Per cent* starting at GS-7 or below . .	59.9	54.7
Attained supergrade: *Years* required	17.8	16.7
Number of bureaus worked in: *Per cent* working in no more than two	72.1	66.6
Service outside the government: *Per cent* who have worked outside the federal government since date of entry	16.3	14.9
Concentration in occupational field: *Per cent* who report all jobs since entry into federal service have been in same occupational field	77.1	76.2

* See Appendix B for a more complete summary of these findings.

ing federal employees in the rendering of such a service as the stimulation of travel from overseas, in the collection of customs, in determining what new foods and drugs may be offered for sale to the public, or in rendering a myriad of other services.

This chapter describes, in terms of day-by-day realities, the nature of the tasks performed by those career civil servants responsible for carrying out the whole or a distinguishable part of a federal program. By abstracting from detailed records of how a representative sample of individuals in such positions spent their working hours during a typical week, it depicts what these individuals do, and with whom they work. Thus, it pictures the nature of "management" in the federal service in fresh and realistic terms.

MANAGEMENT—
THE DISCHARGE OF RESPONSIBILITY

Questions as to Responsibility

What does examination of the day-by-day activities of upper-level career civil servants reveal as to the nature of "management" as it is practiced in the federal government? What does such an examination reveal as to the character of the responsibilities borne by those who direct federal programs?

How broad are their responsibilities? Do they encompass the carrying out of an objective precisely defined in statutes, prevailing plans, or regulations? Or do they extend to the accomplishment of less specifically stated objectives (e.g., the protection of the public against adulterated foods)?

And to whom are these upper-level career civil servants accountable? To a single superior, a boss? Or is the "program manager" accountable in some degree to a number of individuals and groups concerned with the program for which he is responsible?

Illustrative Program Managers

In seeking answers to these questions, consider first, brief summaries of the responsibilities of four typical *program managers*:

—Joe L. Browning, Technical Director of the Navy's Naval Propellant Plant, is a scientist-administrator. He carries out his responsibilities under the supervision of the Commanding Officer. He directs a 2,800-man effort, involving many who hold Ph.D. degrees in the physical sciences. Though not a Ph.D. himself (he has a B.S. in chemistry), he is at home with such terms as "pneumatic mix," "starter cartridge," and "inert diluent process" and is confident of his ability to mould diverse scientific and administrative skills into a productive technical program. He is aware that the ways in which he does this and the standards he maintains are of concern to scientists generally, and are as well subject to review by Congress. As technical director of the Navy's principal propellant organization, Mr. Browning is responsible for the utilization of some $70 million annually (a significant portion of which is for research and development activities), and for the formulation of plans for future programs.

—Robert V. McIntyre, on the other hand, is Deputy Commissioner of Customs for the Treasury Department. His boss is the politically appointed Commissioner of Customs. He is responsible for a clearly distinguishable segment of the work of the Customs Service, i.e., for seeing to it, with the aid of his twenty-eight-man staff, that vessels using United States' ports are properly registered, and that they complete entry and clearance requirements, and pay required tonnage taxes. Mr. McIntyre has also served as a United States Representative to the United Nations' Intergovernmental and Maritime Consultative Organization. He brings to that body his staff's proposals for improving the flow of commerce when they have been approved by his government. Last year, he attended conferences in New York, London, Haifa (Israel), and Mar del Plata (Argentina) to present ideas such as improving the international system for measuring vessel tonnage.

—Joseph O. Fluet, Chief of the Safety Investigation Division in the Civil Aeronautics Board's Bureau of Safety, is one of four division chiefs, all of whom report to a career director in charge of the Bureau. His fellow division chiefs are responsible for providing engineering capabilities, analytical skills, and operational knowledge relative to the Board's safety program (the Civil Aeronautics Board [CAB] is statutorily assigned the responsiblity for determining the causes of civil aircraft accidents). Mr. Fluet and the eighty-four-man staff in his division are the field investigators who, within hours after a major air crash, must be at the site mobilizing inspection and retrieval teams and combing wreckage for clues as to the causes of the disaster. He is responsible for the collection of the vital facts, circumstances, and evidences of aircraft accidents for analysis by the Bureau of Safety which provides the CAB five-member Board with the considered findings enabling it to determine the probable cause of the accident.

—Cornelius K. Call directs the Federal Mediation and Conciliation Service's fifty-nine-member Chicago Region staff under supervision of the Service Director. With the aid of this staff he is responsible for mediating disputes between labor and management groups and for minimizing industrial unrest in the area he serves. His and his staff's success depends largely upon their individual persuasiveness in gaining agreement between the parties on differences over wages, hours, and working conditions. Their success depends as well on their continuing relationships with organized labor and employers in this section of the country.

The textbooks suggest that the manager's tasks are logically pictured in terms of what he does to plan, organize, control, coordinate, evaluate, and appraise the work for which he is responsible. These illustrations of what typical program managers do, and the context within which they do it, suggest that a conceptual analysis of the way they plan, organize, and the like would provide only a one-dimensional and perhaps sterile image of the management process. What is needed is a multi-dimensional reflection of their activities. It is this we strive to present in subsequent sections by picturing the activities for which federal managers are accountable.

Responsibility to Superior

The four men whose activities we have described are each responsible (in the conventional, organizational usage of the term) to an immediate superior or "boss," but this relationship is different for each of the four. It differs because each superior differs in terms of his experience and the understanding of the agency that he brings to the job. It differs because of the style of each individual superior. And both understanding and style will likely differ, as does the origin and hence the experience of the superior.

Joe Browning, for example, has served under a succession of naval officers, each of whom is rotated through the job of Commanding Officer of the Naval Propellant Plant, and most of whom had no prior experience in the administration of research and development laboratories. Robert McIntyre has served under a succession of businessmen and politicians appointed by successive Presidents to serve as Commissioner of Customs. Joe Fluet serves under a career civil servant who learned the field for which he is responsible as he rose through the ranks. And Cornelius Call reports, from his relatively remote field office, to a boss who is also a career civil servant.

Each of the program managers, in their relations with their superiors, has a variety of responsibilities. For example, the Chief of the Division of Timber Management in the United States Forest Service is responsible to the Chief Forester (a career civil servant himself) for selling a stipulated (and large) quantity of publicly owned timber each year. The Camden (New Jersey) District Director of the Internal Revenue Service is responsible to a Regional Commissioner and through him to the national Commissioner for the processing of thousands of tax returns and for the satisfactory performance by his staff of a myriad of incidental auditing, investigative, and informational activities.

But the recorded activities of typical career program managers suggest that their responsibilities to their superiors cannot be effectively depicted by mere description of the functions over which they preside. These responsibilities can more meaningfully be categorized in three interrelated but distinguishable types of relationships.

1. *The upper-level career man serves his superior as an advisor.* The advisory function varies, in the substance of the advice as well as the manner in which it is given, as does the superior's experience and style of operation. Much of the career *program manager's* time is consumed in conferences with the boss, regular meetings with his staff, meetings involving the boss and others from outside the agency, and by sudden calls from the boss to help resolve current problems.

For each superior needs ideas—sometimes urgently. The superior will frequently be under pressure from *his* political superiors or from constituencies (e.g., organized labor) to advance new proposals, to expand the activities of the agency, or to meet current problems. The ideas may take the form of reactions to proposals advanced from without or by the superior himself; thus, the upper-level career man brings the experience of his staff to the superior's aid (though oftentimes not to his liking). Or the career man presents ideas in the form of proposals developed by the staff. In either or both directions the flow of ideas continues—or the agency and its political head suffer.

For example, the Director of the Farmer Programs Division of the Agricultural Stabilization and Conservation Service advised his immediate superior "whether relief could and should be granted to a large number of farmers who were to be penalized (for double cropping their fields) because some (agency) field personnel had given them erroneous information." Similarly, a career man in AID was called in by his boss, the Associate Administrator, to discuss what action should be taken on a request for economic assistance to Ecuador.

Another career program manager, the Chief of the Office of Ship Construction in the Maritime Administration, formulated, in collaboration with other staff members, the prevailing "ship construction-differential subsidy policy" in response to a request from the Secretary of Commerce. And typical of the recurring experience of other program managers is that of the Executive Director of the Federal Power Commission. He—with other key staff members—attends weekly meetings of the five-man Commission "to advise the Commission on matters (orders, opinions, legislative matters, reports to and from other agencies, etc.) pertaining to the regulation of the natural gas and electric industries."

Through such day-by-day meetings and more formal staff conferences, the program manager makes available to the boss not only his personal opinion and advice, but the considered proposals, analyses, and opinions of his staff. Through such means, the program manager exercises his personal influence and brings his staff's work to bear on problems beyond their immediate province. In addition, he is enabled to see his own program in relation to other activities, and to get prompt consideration of the questions he poses to his superior.

But several career program managers were concerned about the time consumed by such conferences and meetings. A branch chief in the Federal Aviation Agency (FAA) estimated that he spent four hours a week "attending large staff or large industry meetings at the request of his superiors in which very few subjects of interest to our branch are discussed." The "sheer movement from office to office and from meeting to meeting," one head of a large research installation claims, takes an inordinate amount of time. One estimated that he "spent approximately two and one-half hours each *en route* between his own office and the main building (in which his superior is located) . . . for (the) purpose of attending conferences."

2. *The upper-level career man serves his superior as an administrator.* Indeed, analysis of program managers' activities suggests that many regard their primary function as that of ensuring the efficient, economic, and timely operation of their staffs.

This means that the program manager devotes much time seeing to it that the men and women who make up his staff are effectively selected, trained, and supervised; that funds are properly spent, and that buildings, equipment, and supplies are productively employed. Administration, reflected in these men's activities, involves many and a variety of details.

For example, the Farm Credit Administration's Chief Examiner "gives continuing attention to finding qualified, professionally trained young people" to replace older examiners who retire. The director of a military research laboratory devoted much time to what he described as "edging out" of the laboratory the least qualified members of his staff. In effect, he told each one that he regarded as incompetent: "The experience you have had here will stand you in good stead . . . in industry. If you don't find a good job in six months, you'll never get started in industry; and moreover, you have learned as much and gone as far as you can here."

An assistant bureau director in the Department of Interior served on a selection committee that developed lists of eligibles for a branch chief position. "I couldn't afford the time," he wrote in explanation, "but the appointee was going to be in my shop . . . I am interested in selecting the best people we can find to do the jobs we must have done. I consider that to be a particularly important responsibility."

To achieve the same end, a branch chief of FAA's Flight Standards Service spent time "boning-up" on the current state of propulsion technology to gain a better basis for planning the additional training required by the twenty-six technical employees in his organization.

Among the numerous administrative details that claim the program manager's time are those involved in seeing to it that his staff has the materials and equipment they need. Obtaining a larger laboratory, more office space, or better equipment may mean successive conferences with agency superiors, representatives of the General Services Administration or the Bureau of the Budget, and suppliers, and even with congressional committees. In any case, the program manager must find the time and sometimes the ingenuity required to satisfy the real needs of his staff (and to be insensitive to the supposed needs).

Administration involves, too, the continual building and improving of the organization. For example, a new department director in the District of Columbia was dismayed to find, when he assumed office, that there were no clear-cut definitions and allocations of responsibilities for the 4,000 individuals that made up the department. He devoted much of the next two years to building a new organization and to preparing manuals that would make known to all what policies guided their work and what was expected of them.

More often the task is that of altering the organizational structure to accommodate changes in program or in the scope of its responsibilities. The Superintendent of the Patent Examining Corps spent three hours, for example, during the week studied, formulating his reactions to a survey team's recommendations for reorganizing the Examining Corps to guide the Commissioner of Patents in deciding what organizational changes should be made.

3. *The program manager is usually held responsible by his superior for maintaining harmonious relations with other govermental agencies, with special interest groups, and with the Congress—its members and its committees.* Achievement of program objectives in most federal agencies requires coordination with other agencies, the support of interested constituencies, and the approval of one or more congressional committees. The task is that of obtaining the requisite coordination, support, and approval, without subordinating the agency or forsaking its objectives as the *quid pro quo.*

For a district director of the Internal Revenue Service (IRS), this task involved "establishing cordial working relationships with professional groups, news media, and officials in state and local agencies." "The attitude of the public towards the Internal Revenue Service," he noted, "materially affects the job of collecting taxes."

For the Director of the Office of the Federal Register, the need to maintain harmonious relationships involved appearances before the national convention of the American Bar

Association. "We are largely dependent," the Director explained, "on the various bar associations, law-library associations, Judiciary Committees of the Congress, law publishers, and bodies like the Administrative Conference of the United States, for realistic and constructive criticism of our publications." And he might have added, "at times for vocal support of our needs."

For the Assistant Commissioner for Materials Management of the General Services Administration's Defense Materials Service (this officer is responsible for acquiring and holding millions of dollars worth of strategic and critical materials for defense and defense-related purposes), the task of obtaining requisite coordination, support, and approval included responses to a score or more calls from members of Congress regarding stockpiles of refractory grade bauxite, uses of industrial diamonds, the level of opium stores, opportunities for upgrading manganese ore contracts, and similar matters.

For many program managers, this task includes frequent appearances before interested groups (e.g., the American Federation of Labor—Congress of Industrial Organizations [AFL–CIO], the National Association of Manufacturers [NAM], or defense industries associations) and before congressional committees. The transient superior—political or military—often looks to a career program manager for a knowledge of "who counts," and, in the words of one veteran civil servant, "to keep the dogs from howling." Thus, the program manager requires skill in negotiating with representatives of other agencies, the pressure groups, and the Congress and, as well, a wide range of acquaintanceships with individuals through whom he can achieve needed collaboration.

Responsibility to and for Subordinates

It may seem contradictory to say that the career program manager is responsible to his subordinates. Yet, analyses of their activities make apparent that career program managers are engaged in a continual effort with their subordinates in planning, in periodically taking stock of accomplishments, in appraising methods and procedures, and thus in gaining concurrence on improvements.

Later on the program manager, perhaps by himself, negotiates on their behalf for funds, manpower, space, or supplies that he has agreed are required. Leadership—as it is seen in the work of a program manager—is not a "one-before-the-group relationship."

Dean Acheson aptly pictured this process in describing the work of the Secretary of State. He wrote that "the sweep of the matters which should go into the making of most judgments is so vast, they are so interrelated and complex, require such depth of particularized knowledge, and call for such synthesis that no single mind or small group of minds is adequate for the quantitative thinking required. Too much must be held in suspension awaiting the catalyst of decision. The organized and disciplined work of many highly trained and experienced minds is necessary."[1]

Planning, as it is carried on in day-to-day practice, is illustrated by the experience of the Director of the Office of Highway Safety in the Department of Commerce. He reported having spent six hours discussing with a special staff task group a plan to name pilot states in which a major effort would be made to improve traffic accident records. That plan grew out of earlier discussions, over nearly a year, with representatives of many other public and private agencies. In contrast, when policies and programs are announced by superiors after little or no consideration with staffs, the program manager is responsible for communicating them to his staff and for aiding the staff to understand and to accept the new policies or programs.

Then follows the task of making a policy operative. The Assistant Administrator for Real Estate Loans in the Farmers Home Administration, for example, had the job of implementing—with respect to his agency—President Kennedy's fair employment order prohibiting discrimination in hiring prac-

[1] Louis J. Halle, *Civilization and Foreign Policy: An Inquiry for Americans*, with an introduction by Dean Acheson (New York: Harper and Row, 1955), p. xviii.

tices of loan recipients. First this involved several extended meetings with representatives of other agencies (to coordinate their efforts), with the Administration's General Counsel (to get advice on legal aspects of implementing the order), and with his key staff members. Then it required that he work closely and frequently with his own staff members to work out internal details.

Once policies are defined and explained, the program manager "keeps in touch" with his staff to ensure that the policies are being carried out and to know when he must redirect staff efforts or adjust originally stated objectives to new developments.

For the Director of an Internal Revenue District, selected to initiate a series of new ways to combat delinquency in the filing of tax returns, this involves spending twelve or more hours each week reviewing accounts, talking with employees about the problems they encountered, accompanying field agents on calls to taxpayers, and meeting with supervisors to exchange views on his observations. For a bureau director in the Civil Aeronautics Board, it is reviewing passenger complaints acted on by staff to determine how better to counsel the staff on more effective handling of such complaints.

Keeping in touch, for most program managers, involves periodic staff meetings. The San Francisco Regional Director of the United States Civil Service Commission relies on staff meetings (occasionally as long as five hours) to bring himself up to date on his staff's work. A Justice Department program manager held twice-weekly staff luncheons "to learn where they stand on pending matters and to give him a 'feel' of staff morale and attitude."

And for some program managers, keeping abreast of the staff requires regular field trips. The Chief Examiner of the Farm Credit Administration, for example, got a firsthand view of his staff's operations by means of a three-day visit to several Farm Credit Banks in Minnesota.

Planning, supervision, and control, as the analysis of these individuals' time suggests, are processes in which many (or most) program managers are involved with their staffs. Thus, the Chief of Federal Trade Commission's Division of Mergers regularly discusses, with his thirty-man legal staff, cases for which they are responsible, to identify those which are delayed in reaching final oral argument before the Commission. Similarly, the Chief of the Justice Department's Antitrust General Litigation Section personally helped prepare legal briefs responding to five separate motions for dismissal of a major criminal case being prosecuted by the Department in a federal court. The importance of this case, she explained, required her personal supplementation of staff efforts.

Some program managers make clear that they perform tasks that could (or should) be handled by subordinates. A division director in the Department of Agriculture explains that he personally prepares a bi-monthly newsletter because it is a "significant means of communication within the Division." He added, "I hope to give larger responsibility for the preparation of this memo to my administrative officer." And the Director of the Office of Development Planning in AID temporarily assumed the duties of one of his division chiefs while the latter was on leave.

Some complain that they handle such routine matters "because the boss expects it of me—he feels that I must see this volume of minutiae to keep on top of the bureau's work, and he wants to see my initials to assure him that he should approve each form or sign each letter." Another declared that: "I find the added burden of requiring my personal signature on every order, amendment to every order, request for special orders, notification of travel, call to active duty, amendment to call to active duty, and uncounted travel vouchers and certifications for first-class travel, excess baggage, and mixed modes of travel an unmitigated nuisance. . . . Signing probably takes less than 10 per cent of (my) time, but it constitutes a serious continual interruption and irritation."

These program managers must understand and communicate (to their staffs) a rich understanding of issues and technology. What program managers actually do involves the grit and grime of substantive problem-solving. Yet, the manager must participate so as to better equip his staff members (oftentimes a large group) to handle succeeding problems with which they will cope. This is the essence of managerial leadership.

Evaluating staff accomplishments consumes perhaps 10 per cent of the typical program manager's time. The Assistant Director for Industrial Research in Interior's Bureau of Commercial Fisheries spent five hours during the week studying, reviewing, and suggesting revisions to a staff report on how better technical assistance might be provided to the Alaskan fishing industry. The Director of the Interstate Commerce Commission's Bureau of Operating Rights spent several hours studying a report by one of the Commission's staff agencies which evaluated the effectiveness of manpower utilization in his bureau. And the Director of the Agriculture Research Services' Crop Research Division chaired a group set up to evaluate the largest of 122 field installations for which he is responsible.

The day-by-day records of federal program managers show that they devote much time to *representing* their staffs. It is the program manager who usually presents, to his superior, staff recommendations relating to program changes, the improvement of methods and procedures, or the desirability of contracting with one supplier or another. It is he who argues for the financial needs of his staff, first to his superiors, then to departmental officials, the Bureau of the Budget, and committees of the Congress.

The program manager is frequently the bridge between the permanent career staff and the more transient—political or military—superior. The Director of the Veterans Administration's Compensation and Pension Service, for example, was requested by the Administrator to analyze and report on the processing of veterans' appeals. This involved learning from his superiors the purpose of the analysis, gathering needed information from his staff, making assignments among them, and assembling their reports. Finally, he reviewed and edited the report drafted by his subordinates in the light of his first-hand knowledge of his superiors' interests.

The program manager's representation extends beyond his

own agency. The Deputy Administrator for Watersheds in the Soil Conservation Service, for example, directs the preparation and presentation of testimony as well as actively participates in certain phases of presenting the testimony before five congressional committees, including the House and Senate Agriculture and Public Works Committees and the Appropriations Committees. His ability to direct and participate in the effective presentation of the Service's fifty watershed work plans sent to congressional committees is crucial to obtaining the funding required for these operations.

The activities of the Director of the Social Welfare Service of the Veterans Administration illustrate still another dimension of this representational function. The Director reported that in 1963 he appeared before ten nation-wide social and health organizations to speak on veterans' welfare problems. During a single week, he spent more than ten hours gathering materials for two such conferences in which he was scheduled to participate.

Responsibility to Peers

The execution of numerous federal programs requires that some program managers meet regularly, if not daily, with managers in other agencies. They meet to coordinate related program elements, to negotiate—with all the specialized expertise their respective staffs represent—the resolution of differences among programs and to develop a consensus that will be acceptable to the Executive Branch, the key constituencies, and the Congress.

The field of water pollution control offers an example. For the "means" of controlling pollution are divided among several agencies including: Agriculture (Forest Service), Army (Corps of Engineers), Interior (Bureau of Reclamation), Health, Education, and Welfare (Water Pollution Control Administration), and Navy (Bureau of Yards and Docks). The actions of one agency may significantly affect the plans of another; e.g., cutting timber to maintain stream flow can alter the design of a public water system.

To cite another example, consider the efforts of the Director of Highways and Traffic for the District of Columbia to reach agreement with representatives of the National Park Service and several other agencies. At the request of the President, they met on four successive days to agree on plans for several major arterial roadways and bridges to carry the Capital's burgeoning commuter traffic. Or consider the continuing task of the Assistant Director of Legislative Reference in the Bureau of the Budget. He regularly brings the representatives of federal agencies together to "work out differences and develop strategy" on bills proposed or introduced by one agency but opposed by the Administration.

To be effective at "running" his program, the manager must be able to persuade those with whom he deals that his interests and program are legitimate and that there is a mutuality of interests among those involved. He must maneuver well with equally powerful and capable managers outside the agency on grounds that are often precarious and shifting.

The program manager's responsibility to his peers often involves responding to requests for advice or help. An official in the Farmers Home Administration, for example, was asked to discuss his agency's use of computers with a peer from another agency. The Scientific Director of the United States Naval Observatory similarly advised representatives of another government laboratory how to make certain scientific calculations.

Program managers commonly complain that they waste time in needless, inter-bureau, inter-agency, and inter-departmental meetings. "There is too much interference by bureaus in each other's business requiring many useless meetings to argue matters which should not be argued . . . ,"one bureau director typically complained.

But the experienced program manager also recognizes that his function involves continuing coordination with his peers in other agencies, the resolution of differences among them, and recurring attempts to reach consensus on issues that mutually affect them. He recognizes, too, a responsibility to be available as a source of information and advice, and the prestige this may bring to him and to his agency. Finally, he understands that, in these peer relationships, his effectiveness as a persuader, a negotiator, and a representative (rather than as a commander) determines his success.

Responsibility to Legislature

The political scientist may contend that the career program manager has no responsibility *to* the Legislature—to its committees or to its members. But the program manager's daily activities indicate that influential members of Congress insist, in practice, upon some qualification of the absolute theory that each and every federal official is responsible to the Chief Executive, and to him and his appointees alone. Disregarding both the semantic problem posed here by different uses of the word "responsibility" and the problem in administrative theory posed by the suggestion of dual lines of authority, there is need for exacting consideration of the relationships that in fact exist and the skills and talents hence required.

The program manager frequently meets with members of Congress to consider specific operating problems, e.g., the appointment of personnel, the letting of a contract, or the location of a particular office. For example, an Assistant Director of the National Park Service met, during the week his activities were under review, to hear a Congressman's views as to suggested policies and guidelines to be followed by the Park Service in providing needed public facilities.

Even more frequently, the program manager replies to correspondence from members of Congress. Some assign to their staff the responsibility for ensuring that letters from the Hill are answered promptly. Others personally review or even prepare answers to many such letters. This they do, one explained, to keep informed of problems in the minds of members of Congress, and as well to ensure that this important correspondence is handled well.

Much time is spent on congressional contacts relative to appropriations and legislation. For example, during the week his activities were studied, the Deputy Commissioner of the Vocational Rehabilitation Administration lunched with the Commissioner to discuss budget strategy prior to meeting with the Chairman and Clerk of the House Appropriations Subcommittee the following day. He estimated that such meetings consume at least twenty days each year. A division director in the Children's Bureau (HEW) explained that activity regarding amendments to a particular bill "required many conferences and telephone calls with bureau, department, and White House staffs to discuss changes and to prepare several drafts of proposed changes in the language of the bill."

Their positions or their knowledge of the program put some program managers in great demand as witnesses before those legislative and financial committees that are important to their agencies. An assistant bureau director in the Bureau of Land Management (Interior) reported: "During the past twelve months, I spent fifteen to twenty days preparing for or testifying at committee hearings on land legislation." And a division director in the Social Security Administration reported: "During legislative consideration of old age, survivors, and disability insurance matters, I spend a good deal of time working with the top-level staff of the department and in appearances before the Bureau of the Budget, Ways and Means Committee, Appropriations Committee, etc. Normally, I am in Washington (his office is in Baltimore) at least twice a week negotiating with constituent organizations in the department or with other departmental organizations in connection with legislative planning."

In summary, most program managers devote effort to preparing or reviewing budget and legislative proposals, or to appearances before intra-departmental committees, the Bureau of the Budget, or one of a number of proper congressional committees. The task of effectively presenting to the Congress a full and reliable basis for its guidance in legislating consumes a substantial proportion of the working year for many program managers. And the long-run success of the career man in this task is materially influenced by his tact, skill, and courage or independence in presenting recommendations to the Congress and in responding to its subsequent inquiries or demands.[2]

Responsibility to Constituencies

Many descriptions of the role of the career civil servant suggest that he is insulated from the influence of the groups that stand to benefit from federal programs—the veterans, labor unions, employers, industry associations, the aged, state and local officials, and the like. They imply that the political executives who serve directly above the career employee serve as an umbrella shielding him from important, powerful, and vociferous constituent groups. Such reasoning implies that the career program manager is generally divorced from the political questions and the "hot" issues.[3]

The reported activities of program managers suggest that these descriptions are unrealistic. Most career program managers are accountable to not one but several constituencies. These constituencies look to public officials for information and advice as to what the government is doing about their problems; often the career program manager is the visible link between their interests and the bureaucracy. In turn, these constituencies support his program when he succeeds in making them recognize a mutuality of interests. The relationship between the constituencies and the federal agency or department is often with and through elected or politically appointed officials; but relationships at other times or at lower levels are often with the career program manager and these relationships are important to his success.

What characterizes the relationships between the *successful* career program manager and the constituent groups which hold him accountable? First, he is recognized by the constituency as being knowledgeable about the program and

[2] Notable examples of unusual success under equally unusual circumstances are provided by Isador Lubin, one-time Commissioner of Labor Statistics; James V. Bennett, retired Director, Bureau of Prisons; Dr. Robert Felix, former Director, National Institute of Mental Health, and Robert Ball, Social Security Commissioner.

[3] Consider, for example, the reasoning of the Second Hoover Commission, 1954.

influential in its operations. The representatives of several private national automotive and highway safety organizations recognized the Director of Highway Safety in the Commerce Department as one such program manager. They requested a meeting so that they might air their pleas for financing various highway safety projects.

Often such contacts with constituent groups are welcomed by the program manager. For he recognizes the need to keep the constituency informed and to maintain such a rapport as will enable him to call on them for support when he needs it. He may personally meet with representatives of their organizations, give speeches to key constituent groups, or, as in the case of a District IRS Director, identify himself with local civic groups and "be available" for community public service chores. A division director in the Veterans Administration cited a speech he gave at a national convention of Jewish War Veterans as illustrative of numerous instances in which he strives to maintain essential relationships. And a Labor Department official reports that he regularly gives speeches before AFL–CIO groups—important constituents of his department.

On other occasions, the constituent representatives may seek out a career manager because he controls a particular program. For example, the Director of the Bureau of Restraint of Trade in the Federal Trade Commission (FTC) spent half of one week negotiating with principals of a large corporation concerned with an FTC ruling which affected their interests adversely. These negotiations were preceded by earlier meetings, phone calls, and personal visits to this bureau director's staff by representatives of the trade association.

Finally, the program manager's relationship is often with several competing constituencies. The interests of the large farm groups, for example, are often opposed by the small and unorganized farmers. The sometimes militant views of the American Legion, a highly organized constituency, are not always shared by all veterans and their families. And the large labor unions unite against a common foe, the employer, yet divide on a host of individual issues involved in their relationships with the Department of Labor.

The program manager weighs and balances such conflicting views on the twin scales of the public interest (which he supports) and these special interests (with which he must cope). These groups provide a helpful focus from which the manager obtains facts and opinions. Often they marshall pressures in support of, or in opposition to, the program manager's efforts. All such activities constitute an important, if complex, element of the environment within which the career man manages in a free society. His is the difficult task of winning recognition from the constituencies, gaining their support, and yet retaining his independence and balanced judgment.

Responsibility to One's Self

It has been written that "a dominant trait of the successful executive is a catholic curiosity." Such curiosity is manifest in the continuing effort of representative program managers to "keep informed as to what is going on" and to expand their own understanding of the range of activities for which they are responsible. When asked why he devoted time to reading most research reports, staff papers, and news releases, a research director in the Department of Agriculture explained that it was secondarily to ensure that they are accurate and concise, and primarily "to keep up with" the work of his staff. Similarly, the director of another division of the same department explained that "reviewing and approving publications of our research results gives me excellent knowledge of the quality, quantity, and progress of the work being turned out by our staff; helps reveal lack of balance in programs; shows me where additional training is required; and helps insure the accuracy and wisdom of the report to reach the public. I review these manuscripts in my office, at home, and on trains."

These several examples illustrate the extra effort required to satisfy this catholic curiosity. That this trait is manifested by many who serve as program managers is reflected by the descriptions of their activities. It is also suggested by the fact that nearly 60 per cent reported that they often work at home (average: 4.2 hours a week).

Careful analysis suggests that one must attribute a portion of their activities (and of this "extra effort") to two other objectives: a desire to advance in terms of personal reputation, and a personal belief in and dedication to the objectives of the program they serve.

Program managers' activities reflect an innate desire and need to grow in their comprehension of their jobs and their capacities. An associate commissioner in the Bureau of Prisons, whose responsibility includes a sizable prison-run textile operation, for example, recognized that he needed to know more about the equipment used in modern textile operations. To gain the increased understanding he regarded as necessary to enable him to carry out a million-dollar modernization of textile operations, he spent much of the week he described in his report visiting cotton mills in North and South Carolina and Georgia.

Similarly, the Director of the Armed Services Technical Information Agency visited a large privately operated physics laboratory to learn more about work being done there on information science and to exchange ideas on information retrieval.

The career program manager is expected to be nonpolitical in the sense that he willingly supports the policies and administers the programs of the Administration in power. Yet, in the speeches he makes, and in the numerous contacts he has with the representatives of constituent groups and even with committees of Congress, he manifests a deep belief in the worthiness of the end-objectives he strives for. The individual who has "grown up with the program" acquires in many instances a deep loyalty, even a sense of dedication to the program (e.g., to the provision of security for aged persons). In his own words, a principal satisfaction that he derives from his work is the conviction that he is doing something worthwhile. This dedication is both an asset and a handicap. It is an asset in his relationships with his staff and with constituent groups. It is an asset in his relationships with the

Congress and with his superiors—but one that may turn into a handicap when political control changes. And it is often a handicap in that it cultivates a narrow parochial point of view.

THE SUBSTANCE OF MANAGEMENT

We have pictured the ways that typical program managers meet six different kinds of responsibilities. These activities, together with the managers' own estimates and records, show somewhat more clearly how these top-level career servants actually manage. They show, for example, that 60 per cent of the program managers' time is spent "managing," that is, in applying the so-called *command skills* of direction, staffing, controlling, planning, and evaluating. But, as their activities have illustrated, program managers spend a significant proportion of their time—more than 20 per cent—in managing by means short of overt direction. These managers seek to persuade others (over whom they have no control) to their viewpoints, and they try to get the best for their programs; they coordinate related activities in their own and other programs. And they, as representatives of their programs and agencies, strive to put their best foot forward before Congress, private industry, and the public. As the next chapter will show, however, they call on their supporting staff managers for these same persuasive skills.

Still, managers are directly involved in the substance of their programs. Those in this study report an average 24.4 hours spent (during the week surveyed) in specialized or functional activities. In contrast, they reported only 4.1 hours spent on general or administrative activities. While most of these activities were accomplished with others, the program managers reportedly put in an average of thirteen hours a week *alone* (perhaps one-third of it at home after working hours) reading, writing, dictating, and reviewing correspondence.[4]

[4] See Appendix B, Appendix Tables 11, 12, and 13.

To what do these findings add up? We believe that six generalizations can be drawn out of this cross-section of federal experience.

1. *Management in the federal service is integrally and inextricably interrelated to an understanding of, and a dedication to, the objectives of the program being managed.*

Dr. Chalmers Sherwin, Deputy Director of Defense Research and Engineering in the Department of Defense, has written of the passing of the "general purpose manager."

> This type of person always has been and always will be essential to many parts of business and government [he wrote]. He is not, however, a suitable person either to operate the law courts, or to direct modern technological enterprises (although he did quite well at managing the relatively simple technical operations of the industrial revolution, particularly operations based on mechanical devices). A lawyer or a businessman can master in a few weeks the essential technical aspects of the operation of a railroad or a busline. But just let him try to rationally guide the development of an inertial guidance system, a laser communications system, or a radical new computer!
>
> The kind of technical knowledge needed in these matters, along with the subtle skills of management which bring out the creative efforts of scientists and engineers, simply cannot be picked up after hours or as part of a job. It can only be obtained one way: by a systematic, thorough technical education plus extensive professional experience in research and engineering. Unfortunately, the lingo of science is easy to pick up. But, as any experienced technical person well knows, there is nothing so depressing as to listen to a "general-purpose" manager using all the right words without real comprehension.[5]

The evidence provided by the record of what career program managers do belies Dr. Sherwin's suggestion that the general purpose manager still is useful in the older and less changing activities of government (e.g., the collection of taxes—and there are those who would question this assertion!). Together, Dr. Sherwin's contention and the record of what career program managers do, challenge a prevailing belief that the manager is a generalist who delegates technical and administrative details and relies on others for the substance of policies and processes, and then focuses his time and energies on interpreting and

[5] *Saturday Review*, August 1, 1964, p. 39 (based on an article which appeared in the *Naval Research Reviews*).

executing these approved policies. The practice of program managers suggests that such an administrator is rare.

The analysis of a complex technical report presented by one's staff, discussions of troublesome problems with members of Congress and interest groups, the gathering of seasoned judgments from highly specialized staff members, and the negotiating with his peers in related fields involve the program manager in the warp and woof of the program. The capacity to represent his staff and to persuade the congressional committee or constituent group often requires not only understanding, but a dedication to the program and its objectives.

It is not surprising, therefore, that most program managers have spent the larger part of their adult careers in the fields in which they are now working. The Director of the Bureau of Restraint of Trade in the Federal Trade Commission, for example, joined the FTC in 1925, after obtaining a law degree. He has worked successively in various fields of legal investigation for 39 years, as an examiner, assistant chief examiner, associate director (Office of Legal Investigations), before becoming bureau director. Similarly, the Director of the Division of Timber Management joined the Forest Service after graduating from college with a degree in forestry in 1925. After starting as a grade GS-5, Assistant Forest Ranger, he served as a Forest Ranger, a member of a Forest Supervisor's technical staff, an Assistant Forester engaged in forest products research, an Assistant Forest Supervisor (general administration), and Assistant Regional Forester, before being promoted to his present job. Both men gained the capacities required in their present posts by dint of long experience in specialized fields.

The program managers' concern with the substance of the program is confirmed by their designation of those activities they engage in that they believe to be most significant. In four of every five instances, the activities that they designated involved substantive (as distinguished from administrative) considerations. Supervising the progress of the case handled by a staff of attorneys, evaluating a technical report on the Alaska fishing industry, or planning a regulatory commission's programs for the coming year are illustrative activities identified by these managers. Such activities require that the program manager be familiar with the technical intricacies of the program he manages.

This dedication to the program is usually associated with a deep sense of responsibility to the whole citizenry. The attitudes of many top-level civil servants are marked by a true feeling of public service, of belief that they are doing something or providing services of great value to all citizens. This attitude is less often observable in the activities of business executives of like rank.

2. *Management is, in substantial part, an entrepreneurial function; it involves the responsibility for continual innovation, i.e., for taking the lead in bringing about changes in legislation, in policy, and in processes of execution.*

Much of the program manager's time goes into activities that are undertaken to develop amendments to existing law, changes in prevailing policies or improvements in processes and procedures. The pressure for change, for growth, and for improvement comes from the day-by-day experience in administration. But simultaneously the pressure for innovation may come from political superiors who strive to fulfill political promises or to achieve political gains, and such pressure will continually come from constituent groups.

The entrepreneurial function of the career program manager[6] is that of having his staff develop the change that is in

[6] The analogous entrepreneurial function of the manager in private business is aptly described by Peter F. Drucker in his book, *Managing for Results* (New York: Harper & Row, 1964), pp. 3–14.

Drucker suggests, later in his book, that this function has, as yet, not been completely realized. He notes: "Managers have become a leadership group in the last two decades largely because they have developed such a discipline for the managerial half of their job: the planning, building, and leading of the human organization of a business. But for the other, the entrepreneurial, half—the half that deals with the specific and unique economic function of business enterprise—the systematic discipline has yet to be evolved. All over the world, executives have committed themselves to management as a discipline. Now they have to commit themselves to purposeful entrepreneurship. Only when entrepreneurship is presented as a discipline and practiced as the specific task that systematically directs resources to economic performance and results, will an educated layman be able to understand what the public interest and then of engineering the consensus required—among staff, the representatives of other executive departments, the Executive Office, constituent groups, and the congressional committees, or such groupings as are required in a particular instance.

3. *Management is the task of continually interrelating forces and groups within and without the agency in the achievement of program objectives.*

The program manager is located at the hub—not the apex— of the groups and forces he must influence if he is to get things done, i.e., if he is to carry out existing law and policy, and is to initiate the continual and progressive change required. He is involved in a never-ending process of adjusting, balancing, and interrelating the views, expectations, and pressures of:

—*superiors*, including his immediate boss, and those "up the line," even perhaps the President;

—*subordinates*, most of them specialists in a number of separate and sometimes little related fields, e.g., the biologist and the lawyer in the Food and Drug Administration;

—*peers*, other career men both within and without the department of which his agency is a part, who are responsible for parallel programs and compete with him for funds and for the support of the Executive Branch, constituencies, and the Congress; concurrently, they are partners in meeting over-all objectives of the Executive Branch;

—*advisors and supporting specialists*, outsiders who contribute economic, scientific, public relations, or other viewpoints deemed related to the agency problems and to the achievement of agency objectives;

—*members of Congress* who represent the views of constituents and who, as members of key substantive or fiscal committees, can significantly affect the administrator's batting average in getting needed legislation through or in obtaining requisite funds;

---

business—industrial society's economic organ—is trying to do, and to respect what it is doing. Only then can society truly accept that business is a rational pursuit and that the executive in business has an important contribution to make." (P. 227.)

—*representatives of special interest groups* (e.g., labor, industry, agriculture, and veterans organizations) who seek to influence the administrator and the agency by plying their special interest wherever they can gain an audience.

And importantly, the manager must reconcile these many obligations with his own personal sense of responsibility to himself. The process of management, in terms of this reconciliation, involves discovery or development of the solution, policy, or action which will serve the public interest, maximize concurrence among the several constituent groups, and yet leave the manager with the conviction that he has acted according to his own highest sense of right.

The task is similar to the role Marya Mannes pictures for the conductor of a private orchestra. He is responsible as an artist for relating the contributions of pianists, flutists, violinists, and others, while at the same time he is occupied with harmonizing the demands of the musicians' union and his board of trustees and with stimulating the interest and approval of the press, of prospective customers in other cities, and of contributors wherever he can find them.[7] Leonard Sayles has identified thirteen similar groups or forces with which the business executive must cope.[8]

4. *Management is essentially a process of negotiation and persuasion; it is, at the most, only partially a process of command.*

In developing a solution, a policy, or an action that will serve the public interest and maximize concurrence,

> ...who has authority over whom is a moot point. The balance of power, of status and influence tends to be ambiguous. These types of interaction, therefore, require enormously more personality abilities than did jobs under simpler kinds of technologies. Much more skill and time has to be given to negotiation-like behavior patterns, to interviewing,

[7] Marya Mannes, *But Will It Sell?* (New York: J. B. Lippincott & Co., 1964), pp. 238–239.

[8] He includes among these groups those ". . . for whom he is doing work, . . . to whom he, in turn, contracts out work, . . . from whom he gets parts, materials, or services . . . who control the access to equipment, space, and other resources . . . to whom he will send what he has processed . . . who are doing things in other parts of the organization that directly or indirectly impinge on his activities." "Executives Need This Skill," by Leonard P. Sayles, *Nation's Business*, © August, 1964, p. 49.

and a whole host of skills that are the opposite of the smothered individual which critics of large corporations tend to fret about.[9]

In the federal service even more than in private enterprise, these "personality abilities" are of prime importance. For no matter how great are the career civil servant's professional attainments, no matter how long is his service or how rich his experience, and no matter how clearly his competence is recognized, he always occupies a secondary or even tertiary position in the federal service. If J. Edgar Hoover has achieved a primary role in the determination of what policies shall govern and how federal law enforcement activities shall be carried out, he constitutes the exception that proves a valid and generally prevailing rule. The career civil servant, while he may be clearly responsible for the conduct of a particular service, is the subordinate of a politically appointed superior who is expected to approve the policies that shall prevail and to oversee the manner in which they are executed.

5. *Management is primarily a group process; it is seldom the task of an all powerful individual working alone.*

The activities which consume a major portion of the program manager's time (perhaps three-fifths of all his working hours), and most (over 75 per cent) of the activities which he regards as "most significant," are group activities, i.e., conferences, meetings, and group discussions. The program manager spends a minor part of his time alone. He has relatively little time to focus his talents and experience alone on the problems for which he is responsible, little time to read, to write, and to deliberate.

This characteristic of the program manager's activities derives in large part from the fact that the career civil servant is often only responsible for a part of a total governmental effort. For example, the career official in the Department of Agriculture responsible for shipping surplus agricultural commodities to the developing countries provides but a portion of the aid the United States makes available to these countries. Technical experts, machinery, equipment, and perhaps loans

[9] *Ibid.*, p. 50.

may be provided by AID, while military equipment and military advisors may be supplied by the Department of Defense. These activities must be carried on in consonance with objectives set by the State Department if the resources provided by each of these separate programs are to accomplish this country's foreign policy ends.

The decisions made by the program manager arise far more often out of consultation than out of his single-minded judgments. The decision usually reflects the informed and debated views of those involved in the problem. It may, at times, represent the abdication by the program manager of the responsibility for making the decision to the will of a majority.

6. *Management demands of the manager skill in communication, perhaps to a greater degree than any other skill.*

The Deputy Treasurer of the United States, who is responsible for an organization which provides general banking services and related activities for the entire federal government, wrote of his own job: "The talking, conferring, dictating, reading, and writing constitute a continuing communication with superiors, subordinates, personal staff, equals in other bureaus and departments, Congressmen and their assistants, committees of Congress, members of the general public, and the press."

In other words, the program manager's accomplishment, this official indicates, depends largely on his ability to communicate with others—in writing and orally—to gather needed facts and views; to instill subordinates with the confidence that he understands the problems they are attempting to resolve and the programs they are engaged in; to persuade these subordinates of the wisdom of following and supporting his leadership; to sell his program to peers, bosses, interest groups, Congress, and the public; and to win the support of powerful and interested groups for his agency's programs.

This requires a large capacity for putting scientific and economic jargon into terms that the boss, a Congressman, or a newspaper reporter can understand. The possession or lack of this capacity can make or break a program by itself.

Of special importance to the American form of government is the ability of the program manager to translate the program to and to educate his politically appointed boss. Indeed, it is the only way the political appointee learns about his own department—and his learning is of vital importance.

Finally, the program manager must manifest an ability to sense the reactions of each of the groups with which he deals. It is by these reactions that he measures his accomplishments; for he is usually denied the neat quantitative measures that guide the private business executive.

James A. Perkins, the able president of Cornell University, aptly described this needed communication skill in response to the question: "How do you tell whether you're doing well in your job?"

> From the reactions of the public with whom I deal, [he replied]. If the various boards you deal with start asking a lot of small questions or arguing small points, you can figure you're doing something wrong.
>
> Or if you find yourself repeatedly under attack from the faculty, or from the students (I pay attention to the student newspaper), or if many alumni are restive—you're in trouble.
>
> On the other hand, if these people say—or give the impression—that they're kind of pleased, then you feel you're doing all right. You have to trust your personal radar to a great extent.[10]

So it is with the federal program manager. He will often have quantitative measures he can use to claim accomplishment. But in the end, he must possess that communication skill that Perkins describes as his "personal radar" to measure his accomplishment continually.

[10] "An Informal Call on James A. Perkins Far Above Cayuga's Waters," by William McCleery, *University* (a quarterly publication of Princeton University), © March, 1965, p. 19.

Chapter III

THOSE WHO PROVIDE MANAGERIAL SUPPORT

THE INTERNAL REVENUE SERVICE includes a staff of more than 60,000 persons. This staff is responsible for collecting some $80 billion in federal income taxes from individual Americans and from United States corporations. The leadership of this organization provides an illustration of the complex of human skills required to run a large federal agency. And it affords a pragmatic picture of the variety of supporting staff managers that are required.

At the top there are two men, the Commissioner, a presidential appointee, and the Deputy Commissioner. The incumbent Deputy Commissioner is a career employee with twenty-seven years of service. The Commissioner and Deputy Commissioner are assisted by a top management team which includes two Assistants-to, a Chief Counsel, six Assistant and eight Regional Commissioners, and fifty-eight District Directors. Some of these, like the Commissioner and the Deputy Commissioner, are *program managers*.

The Assistant Commissioner for Compliance, Donald W. Bacon, offers an illustration. Aided by six division directors, he heads a field staff of more than 36,000 employees. Each division director is responsible for a distinguishable program or sub-program, for example, the collection of alcohol and tobacco taxes, or the auditing of taxpayers' returns.

The eight Regional Commissioners of IRS provide examples of individuals responsible for carrying out programs within a particular geographical area. They direct the efforts of fifty-eight district offices and seven service centers in the collection and enforcement of our tax laws.

But several of those on the IRS top staff do not bear responsibility for the accomplishment of substantive tax programs. These individuals provide management services essential to the operation of this large and far-flung organization; they illustrate the activities of those top-level federal civil servants who serve as *supporting staff managers.*

The Assistant Commissioner for Administration, Edward F. Preston, provides a wide range of management services. He is assisted by five division chiefs, each responsible for a separate "service."

—*Facilities Management.* Bruce McNair, age sixty, grade GS-16, with twenty-nine years of federal service, is the Service's real estate manager. His properties amount to nearly 11 million square feet of office buildings, including a small office of 66 square feet in Albany, Missouri, and the twenty-one story District Office (the Service's largest) in mid-town Manhattan. Among other things, he is responsible for the publications branch which last year devoured some 400 carloads of paper and printed 1.65 billion forms and publications!

—*Fiscal Affairs.* Gray W. Hume, age fifty-three, Fiscal Management Officer for IRS, also grade GS-16 and a long-term federal servant (thirty-one years), handles the IRS budget of more than $550 million per year. Mr. Hume and his staff of eighty-four are relied upon by the Commissioner to assemble a "salable" budget package—i.e., one that Congress will accept—and to see that, once appropriated, the funds will be properly spent in financing approved programs.

—*Personnel.* A. J. Schaffer, grade GS-16, age forty-nine, with twenty-eight years of federal service, is responsible for the quality of men and women recruited. As Personnel Officer, he and his 118-man staff seek to bring into the service, and provide development opportunities for, such diverse individuals as mathematical statisticians, foresters, digital computer programmers, tax law specialists, intelligence specialists, general administrative officers, and middle-level managers.

—*Public Relations.* Joseph S. Rosapepe, grade GS-16, age fifty-one, a relative newcomer to federal service (six years), is the Service's Public Information Officer. He and his twenty-seven man staff strive to enlist the mass media in support of the Service's enforcement efforts, inform taxpayers of their responsibilities, and combat unfavorable news stories about the Service and its employees. Simultaneously he is responsible for continually building a "conscience" among IRS employees. His goal is that every contact with the taxpayer and the public improves the image of the Service.

—*Employee Training.* George T. Reeves, grade GS-16, age forty-two, sixteen years in public service, is the IRS Training Director. He and his staff of ninety-three conduct eighty separate training programs for Service employees. These offer specialized instruction in numerous areas such as auditing techniques, the application of the Internal Revenue Code, speedreading for punchcard operators, as well as courses designed to develop supervisory and managerial skills.

The Assistant Commissioner for Planning and Research provides the Commissioner and the Deputy Commissioner with still another form of specialized service. William H. Smith, with four division directors and a 300-member staff, develops and maintains a Service-wide financing plan. This staff carries on research, produces statistics to reveal the workings of our tax system, and develops systems to support long-range planning activities

Still, there are other forms of supporting staff assistance, available to top federal program managers, *not* reflected in this particular group of IRS managers. For example:

—*Congressional liaison officers* in many agencies provide vital links between the program manager and the Hill. Throughout the bureaucracy, some fifty of such individuals have full-time liaison duties with Congress; many more do the job on a part-time and informal basis.[1] Some large departments have more than one of these liaison people at the top and in those departments where the legislative load is heavy or the stream of inquiries from Congress is high, many other people—who do *not* bear the title of Congressional Liaison—are apt to be involved in maintaining liaison with the Congress.

—*Procurement officers*, specialists in buying large volume and complex items, are required in most larger bureaus and federal departments. These specialists develop purchasing policies, let procurement contracts, evaluate contractor performance, and audit contract provisions.

Most supporting staff managers provide a particular service in an identifiable function or specialty (e.g., fiscal management, personnel, inspection, planning) to one or several program managers. There are two exceptions to this generalization. These, the deputies and assistants-to, provide a more flexible and often more personal kind of support.

—*Deputies*. Slightly less than one-tenth of the top-level *supporting staff managers* serve as deputies to program managers. Of these, the majority specialize in a functional field such as procurement or administration. A sizable minority—including the Deputy Commissioner of the Internal Revenue Service— operates essentially as the alter ego of the boss, carrying a substantial, even though not the ultimate, responsibility for program accomplishment.

For example, the Deputy Director of the Bureau of International Commerce (Department of Commerce) aids the Director on the whole range of his job. During the single week studied, he met with the United States Ambassador to Thailand, a group of foreign students, and several industrial representatives; attended a business luncheon with the Secretary and a country director in the AID program; discussed problems

---

[1] *The Congressional Quarterly* identified, in 1962, some forty-six men and women then serving as congressional liaison officers. About one-third were supergrade employees; half had been active in Democratic politics in various capacities, eight were particularly active in the 1960 Kennedy campaign; and virtually all were between thirty and fifty years of age. (Issue of March 16, 1962, p. 439.)

of office space allocation with the Assistant Secretary for Administration; and worked out details of some technical exhibits with the staff of the departmental Publications Office.

Certain identifiable characteristics are common to all or most of the deputies' jobs.[2] These include:

> —advising the boss (either with respect to a particular function or on an across-the-board basis);
> —acting for the boss in his absence;
> —relieving the boss of burdens that he cannot readily delegate to lower levels in the organization;
> —concentrating on special problems that require an organization-wide purview, acccss to the boss, and a capacity to speak *for* the boss.

—*Assistants-to.* Nearly 20 per cent of the supporting staff managers are assistants-to. More than half serve their bosses primarily in one specialized area (e.g., engineering, communications, international relations). The Special Assistant to the Commanding General of the Army's Test and Evaluation Command, for example, serves as "the top expert advisor and consultant to the Commanding General . . . in all engineering and scientific matters related to the mission of the Command."

Perhaps 40 per cent or more of all assistants-to are not confined to a single function, but aid the boss in the whole range of his activities. The Executive Assistant to the Secretary of Labor, for example, is in charge of the Secretary's personal office and serves as the liaison between the Secretary and the Department.

Some assistants-to handle a broad range of agency problems, but have an area to which they devote special attention. The Assistant Deputy Attorney General in the Justice Department fulfills such a role. He occupies:

[2] Dr. David S. Brown, writing in the *Civil Service Journal*, cites six difficulties that often attend the deputy position. These include: (1) difficulties in dividing the workload between the boss and the deputy, (2) an additional and often unneeded hierarchial level added to the organization, (3) a similarly unneeded reduction in the span of control of the top managers, (4) duplication of effort and overlap of duties, (5) uncertainty and confusion among those working at lower levels, and (6) disagreement and occasionally open conflicts between the boss and the deputy. *Civil Service Journal*, October-December, 1964, pp. 9–12.

a staff position in which I receive assignments from and report directly to the Attorney General and to the Deputy Attorney General. These assignments relate to any activity in which the Department of Justice may engage, but there is emphasis on congressional liaison and legislation.

In contrast to the deputy, the assistant-to usually is a younger man performing a less powerful role. He has no responsibility for command, is not empowered to act for the boss, and serves as a Man Friday to the boss, undertaking as the job requires a tremendous variety of activities. Yet certain common responsibilities are borne by most men in such jobs. Often the assistant-to acts as:

—*A Channel of Communication.* He serves as a means of contact between the boss and the bureau chiefs, branch chiefs, and regional officials who report to him; as a conveyor of the boss's decisions; a relayer of the subordinates' reactions and reports; and a coordinator of those who must implement these decisions. To those outside the department, the assistant-to is a buffer protecting his boss. He works to sell his boss's ideas, to hear gripes from the public and from special groups, and to filter out the important from the trivial.

—*The Doer of Special Projects.* Following the Cuban crisis, one of the IRS Commissioner's two assistants-to spent full time trying to work out tax arrangements for those companies who volunteered to give needed supplies to Castro in exchange for the prisoners he held. This use of assistants-to occurs especially when the project requires the coordination of two or more subdivisions of the organization, and is of special concern or urgency to the boss.

The assistant-to, particularly because of his association with his boss, *can be* very influential. His position often enables him to know the boss's preferences on many matters. He can, therefore, push ideas put forth by other staff people, if he chooses, or he can turn a deaf ear and fail to put ideas with which he disagrees before the boss.[3]

---

[3] The role of the assistant-to—in business, the military, the federal government and municipal government—is ably explored by Thomas H. Whistler in "The Assistant-to in Four Administrative Settings," *Administrative Science Quarterly,* September, 1960, pp. 181–216. Mr. Whistler notes, in addition to the characteristics above, that the assistant's appointment to the job "is dependent on a mutual personal liking between himself and his chief."

WHAT THE STAFF MANAGER'S ACTIVITIES
REVEAL OF HIS RESPONSIBILITIES

So far we have done no more than identify the variety of supporting staff specialists that surround a program manager within the federal service.[4] The mere identification of these supporting staff specialists does not, however, depict their activities. Nor does it reveal the nature of the supporting staff work and of the responsibilities borne by the *supporting staff manager*. In succeeding sections of this chapter, we will declare the nature of the activities provided by these individuals, describe the relationships that obtain between them and their program manager bosses, and indicate how their responsibilities differ from those of the program managers. As a preface to that depiction of what supporting staff managers do, we present Table 2.

Responsibility for the Specialty

The large majority of supporting staff managers are responsible for a particular function—e.g., personnel administration, budgeting, procurement or congressional liaison. All of the managerial specialists, the majority of the deputies, and at least half of the assistants-to reflect in their daily activities (and in their career paths) a concentration on a specialized function. And these men report that a majority of their working hours are spent on activities directly involving their specialized skill.

Consider Victor Fischer's experience as an assistant-to in the Housing and Home Finance Agency (HHFA). The specialized

---

[4] A recent survey of some 300 top corporation executives commented on this need for business executives to relate to their staffs: "Staff experts . . . will proliferate, and dealing with them—learning to understand what they are talking about—will demand more of a chief executive's time." One corporation president noted: "The new executive . . . needs greater skill and diplomacy in dealing with people. We are in the midst of a vast social revolution, and the relationship between employer and employees, and between the various steps in the organization are already handled on a different basis from what was common a few years ago." From "The Changing American Executive," *Dun's Review and Modern Industry*, January, 1964, p. 60 and p. 40.

Table 2. A Profile of the Supporting Staff Manager Compared
with All Upper-Level Civil Servants*

	Supporting Staff Manager	All Upper-Level Civil Servants
Average age	50.5	52.0
Marital status	97% Married	96% Married
Education: *Per cent* of college graduates with at least one advanced degree	49.0	60.1
Field of study: *Per cent* listing law, economics, or engineering	36.0	43.6
Entry into federal service: *Per cent* entering prior to 1940	46.9	50.9
Length of federal service: *Per cent* with more than twenty years	59.9	59.9
Starting grade: *Per cent* starting at GS-7 or below . .	55.8	54.7
Attained supergrade: *Years* required	16.9	16.7
Number of bureaus worked in: *Per cent* working in no more than two	51.0	66.6
Service outside the government: *Per cent* who have worked outside the federal government since date of entry	12.9	14.9
Concentration in occupational field: *Per cent* who report all jobs since entry into federal service have been in same occupational field	71.1	76.2

* See Appendix B for a more complete summary of these findings.

skill he brings to his job as Assistant Administrator for Metropolitan Development is derived from graduate training in city planning and some twelve years experience, mostly in local and state government. During the week studied, he applied that experience in such activities as:

—analyzing, with officials from the American Municipal Association, the Bureau of the Budget, and the Advisory Commission on Intergovernmental Relations, the role of the federal government in metropolitan development;

—discussing inter- and intra-agency planning programs and coordinating policy matters with his opposite number in the Urban Renewal Administration;

—conferring on transportation planning problems with members of the Bureau of Public Roads and the Urban Renewal Administration planning staff;

—discussing Alaska's planning efforts for housing renewal with a former Executive Director of the Alaska State Housing Authority;

—refining, with others, HHFA's role in coordinating programs to meet the urban impact needs in the Cape Kennedy area.

John L. McHugh's experience (Assistant Director for Biological Research in the Department of the Interior, a Ph.D. in zoology) suggests that the scientist may concentrate even more extensively on activities in his field.[5] In defining the qualities he would seek in looking for his own replacement, Mr. McHugh says he would look for one who had "as broad an education in science as possible, with emphasis on the ocean and its living resources, with a Ph.D. degree or equivalent." In this job, a man should have, he believes, "experience in as many phases of the fishing industry as possible," and a "knowledge of the operation of fishing boats and gear, and processing plants." And he must possess additional qualifications. Mr. McHugh identifies these additional qualities, this "extra something," as including familiarity with "the social political aspects of resource utilization and management"; the ability to communicate, that is, an ability to "put scientific information in simple, clear, and concise form, either written or oral"; the physical capacity "to work long hours under pressure without losing patience"; an ability to work with others of a wide variety of backgrounds and educational levels"; and finally, a "sympathetic understanding of foreign customs and points of view."

[5] During the week surveyed, for example, he:

—reviewed reports on technical aspects of oceanography;

—discussed with the Chief of the Branch of Marine Fisheries plans for a new oceanographic laboratory;

—considered, with a branch chief, the advisability of including additional specialized research area in the National Oceanographic program;

—met with the Associate Bureau Director to discuss a letter regarding "the control of marine fouling organisms in intakes of saline water conversion plants";

—reviewed a technical presentation he was scheduled to make before a symposium sponsored by the Federal Council for Science and Technology on the subject of biological oceanographic research;

—gathered and edited materials for a statement on pesticides to be submitted to the Deputy Assistant Secretary for Fish and Wildlife;

—prepared information for the Secretary on the state of fisheries in Tanganyika.

In short, the positions held by most supporting staff managers at these upper levels are the culmination of career-long efforts to advance in a particular kind of activity. Two-thirds of those surveyed reported that *all* jobs since their entry into federal service have been in but one occupational field. Here are two typical cases:

> The Director of the Contract Audit Policy Division in the Comptroller's Office of the Secretary of Defense entered federal service in 1950 as Deputy Comptroller to the Economic Cooperation Administration (ECA) mission to England. A year later, he joined the Department of Defense (DOD) as an internal auditor, later transferring to the General Accounting Office and subsequently returning to DOD. Over 13 years, he has performed as an auditor in progressively more important auditing posts.
>
> The Chief of the Installation and Materiel Division in the Federal Aviation Agency's (FAA) Eastern Region has been engaged in construction work for thirty years. For six years he served as a project engineer and superintendent of construction with the National Park Service. He continued this experience in the Civil Aeronautics Authority where he designed and constructed airports and navigational facilities. Subsequently, in FAA, the CAA's successor agency, he is responsible for the design, construction, and installation of aids to air traffic control and air navigation.

These men began their careers with some qualification or aptitude for a field of specialized activity. They gradually developed greater competence, expertness, and—in many cases—supervisory ability within the bounds of this specialized activity. In the words of one observer: "The career paths of many federal bureau chiefs are grooves of specialization, deepening as they advance."[6]

---

[6] William C. Thomas, *Public Administration Review*, Vol. 21, No. 1, Winter, 1961, pp. 13–14. Reporting on a study of ninety bureau chiefs in the New York City government (of which fifty-seven were line and thirty-three staff), this author comments: "If it is true as a general proposition that administration grows more common with higher echelons and that one does not need to have knowledge of 'something' to administer that something, it would be logical to expect to find some evidence of increasing leakage from the deep specialized career channels to outside positions as careers advanced to higher bureaucratic levels. None of any consequence whatsoever was found. Instead, a proliferation of pockets, or cones—bureaus—was found, within which the men selected at successively higher echelons tended to be the possessors of more and more particular kinds of experience and, presumably, particular knowledge and skill." Reprinted by permission of the American Society of Public Administration.

One may ask, When does a groove become a rut? For some supporting staff managers take a zealous attitude toward their function and reflect little appreciation of the need to adapt their techniques and their organizations to the requirements of the program for which they provide administrative support.

> One staff manager who heads up a 130-member staff, of which "most . . . are engaged in providing computing services," remonstrates about "administrative-oriented activities dictated from above," and of having to devote time to "regularly scheduled discussions of . . . program affairs [that] are only remotely related to the work of this section." These activities, he contends, divert "scarce capability to sterile, unnecessary, obstructive, bureaucratic system-generated administrative exercises."

> One Personnel Director spends time interviewing potential recruits for top-level jobs, counseling with program managers on personnel problems, meeting with union representatives, discussing government-wide policies at the Civil Service Commission with other departmental personnel officers, or exchanging experiences with other personnel officers (e.g., on particular training programs or the use of "exit interviews"). The other half of his time goes to "running the shop"—meeting with his immediate staff, supervising the work of his division heads, evaluating their performance, and assembling the resources they need to get the job done.

Responsibility to Superior

Supporting staff managers view their obligation to the boss in different ways according to their relative roles in the organization and their distance from the throne. The assistants-to tend to think of this relationship in personal terms. They speak of their obligation to "provide maximum assistance to the Director," to "relieve him of some of the heavy burden he carries," or to try to "keep at least some of these people (visitors) off the Director's back." This function of protecting the boss is accepted by other supporting staff managers as essential but regarded as irksome and time-consuming.[7]

---

[7] For example, one wrote that he met on "Tuesday with . . . from San Francisco. This fellow is trying to establish a . . . activity in California and the Director was decent enough to talk with him one day—both of us spent several hours with him a month ago. This was a follow-up visit; there have been several letters since; the man is an idiot, and I have tried to get him off the Director's and my backs. Because we are civil servants, we dern well have to be decent to such people, and it does take time."

Supporting staff managers, other than the assistants-to, think of their relationship to a superior not in terms of personal duty, but in terms of their obligation for the development of a special function within the agency, to see to it that their specialty provides the full measure of aid of which (they are convinced) it is capable. The descriptions by two managerial specialists of their jobs are revealing:

> The Deputy Chief of Administration for the Forest Service states: "I am responsible for all matters dealing with finances, work schedules, personnel, information activities, administrative services, and coordination of inspection and internal audit activities. As a member of the Chief's staff, I am responsible for advising him and frequently acting for him and other Deputy Chiefs on Forest Service activities involving administration."

> And the Director of the Office of Management Services in the Department of Agriculture wrote: "I direct the planning, development, and administration of a management support program for seventeen of the Department's agencies. The service areas are a program of budget and finance, a personnel program, an information program, and other support programs such as records and communication, space, procurement and contracting. In addition, there is the major role of performing or supervising general management analysis, systems, advisory and consulting activities in support of the substantive and technical programs of the agency served."

In effect, these men (and others) say: I am responsible for providing a designated service throughout the agency or department to all who require that service. The comments of these men, as well as their practices, suggest that they must see to it that the service is used. The supporting staff manager usually regards himself as being responsible (in the sense of being obligated to provide the service) to a number of bosses, i.e., division chiefs, bureau heads, assistant secretaries, and the like. Nominally and finally, he may be responsible to the head of the agency, but the individual staff manager—the budget director, the procurement officer, or the information officer, for example—generally holds himself accountable to others "in the line" for the availability and excellence of the service for which he is responsible—and for ensuring that they make use of the service.

Responsibility to and for Subordinates

The staff manager's supervisory responsibilities differ from those of the program manager in three important respects:

—He directs the activities of fewer employees (about one-third as many) than does the program manager. Most supporting staff managers supervise staffs of their own, some of them sizable.[8] Deputies are less likely to have large staffs, and assistants-to may have only a secretary.[9]

—The employees he directs constitute a more homogeneous group than those of the program manager. The supporting staff managers' aides are usually each concerned with related aspects of a single function; the supporting staff managers' span of control, in this sense, is limited. In contrast, the program managers' subordinates include other line officials, staff managers of several functions, and various other people who act as personal staff.

—Finally, the staff manager is engaged in developing specialists. His effectiveness as a supporting staff manager depends upon his helping them become better specialists and in training them to handle relationships with the program people they serve.[10]

In a real sense, the staff manager is responsible both *to* and *for* his staff. His obligations *to* his staff revolve around his need to build and maintain his workforce. The variety of everyday chores that this involves is indicated by these illustrations:

The Chief of an Army computer services unit employing 133 people met with his own staff, his parent organization's administrative expert, and some outside "correspondents" to try to map out a program for recruiting some competent, trained mathematicians and statisticians (at master's degree levels) for the unit.

The Chief Scientist in a Personnel Research Office met individually with several members of his staff to discuss "technical, methodological, and research problems" and to give personal guidance to them in their work.

---

[8] For example, the Director of Procurement in the Post Office Department's Bureau of Facilities supervises 1,500 people. The managerial specialists whose activities were studied supervised an average of 242 employees.

[9] The average number of employees supervised by the deputy-assistant-to group in this study was 188. This average is probably higher than the median since a few deputies reported fairly large staffs, and several assistants-to reported none at all.

[10] These differences enable supporting staff managers to spend somewhat less time on staff supervision than do program managers. The staff managers in this study reported that approximately one-eighth of their time is spent on supervising staff; the program managers reported that a slightly greater portion of their time is invested in such activities.

The Comptroller of a Defense agency discussed his role in "training staff to dig out detailed facts behind a problem." He noted that they were "too ready to accept someone's verbal explanation rather than spend time documenting [the] case with facts and figures and then reasoning out the best solution." He noted: "There is usually no set of guidelines, rules, or procedures to follow—each problem usually requires special handling or treatment—we are having to 'write the book' as we go and it takes time we don't have."

And the Chief of the Employee Programs Division in the Air Force used a private luncheon for "an open, frank, two-way discussion" with an employee "who was very able and capable" but who had "problems that were beginning to affect his job performance."

In short, the supporting staff manager is responsible *for* his employees in that he directs their efforts, gives substantive counsel on matters related to their work, prods them when they need it, and tries to be sure that their work is of the highest quality they can attain. These are the commonly recognized responsibilities of the supervisor for his subordinates. But analysis of what supporting staff managers do indicates that they have an added and substantial obligation to their subordinates. It is that of representing them and of "selling" their ideas and recommendations. The supporting staff group's accomplishment depends upon the acceptance by others of recommendations it makes, and indeed of the group itself as an effective aide to the program manager. That acceptance depends in major part upon the supporting staff manager's ability at selling his subordinates' recommendations and the need for their services to the program managers and others. This means that in day-by-day practice the supporting staff manager spends perhaps another eighth of his working time in dealing with others as the voice of his subordinates.

Responsibility to Congress

Each agency or department of the Executive Branch carries on a variety of continual relationships with the Congress. Analysis of what the supporting staff managers do makes clear that the responsibility for many of these relationships falls on these men and women. Many supporting staff managers and their staffs spend hundreds of hours each year answering questions or providing assistance requested by members of Congress and their staffs. In general, what the supporting staff managers do to maintain effective relationships can be categorized as follows.

First, the deputy or assistant-to with general responsibility, in the words of one assistant-to, is "up to his neck in congressional relations." Recall, for example, the Assistant Deputy Attorney General whose work involved an "emphasis on congressional liaison and legislation." These individuals, by virtue of their backgrounds, abilities, and rapport with their bosses, carry the responsibility for a great miscellany of relationships—ranging from a simple request for information to the conveying of a confidential viewpoint that the Congressman is anxious to get across to the boss.

Second, the program manager relies upon his budget officer to maintain harmonious and effective relationships with the appropriations subcommittees that appropriate funds for the program. To establish this relationship, the budget officer sees to it that bureau heads, division chiefs, and others effectively develop and present their needs for financial support to the congressional appropriations committees (and before that to the Bureau of the Budget). It means that he will arrange for other staff men to appear before the committee; for example, the Chief of Army's Installations Management Division spends twenty-five to thirty days a year as "a supporting witness before congressional committees." It means also that the budget officer must help his superior understand the mood and interests of the congressional committee. Sometimes, understanding the mood—and convincing Congress of it—is a painstaking process. One departmental budget officer commented on his efforts to develop his boss's opening statement:

> Material for this statement was obtained from bureaus and offices and from the Secretary's aides. I did the actual writing of the first draft myself, for I had to ensure that it touched on the problems I knew members of the Committee were concerned with. The statement was revised four times before it was put into final shape and involved personal conferences with the Secretary and with other Secretarial officers.

Much of the writing of the first draft was done at home during evenings and weekends. Somewhere between thirty and forty hours were devoted to this 25-page statement over a period of four weeks. This is probably too much time, but it was necessary because of the need to obtain such a wide assortment of clearances.

The critical role played by budget officers is noted by one student of the budget process:

Relationships of confidence between agency personnel and subcommittee staff are also vital and eagerly sought after. Contacts between subcommittee staff and budget officers are often frequent, intensive, and close. Frequency of contacts runs to several times a day when hearings are in progress, once a day when the bill is before the committee, and several times a month during other seasons.

The office of the budget official [during appropriations time] turns into a complex communications center in which the phone is always ringing and a constant flow of information is coming in and being sent out.[11]

Third, the personnel director (particularly in the large and expanding agency) is called upon to handle many inquiries as to potential jobs for the constituents of members of Congress—by mail, by telephone, and in person. In addition, as the Director of Personnel for the Department of Agriculture reported was his experience, personnel directors are regularly called upon to appear before the House or Senate Committees to testify as to the efficiency with which their departments are using their manpower. In the recent past, the directors of personnel were called to appear before the Internal Security Committee of the Senate to satisfy its members as to the adequacy of their efforts to ensure the loyalty of all workers.

Fourth, the General Counsel often bears the brunt of the responsibility for working with legislative committees on the drafting or amending of legislation. This, depending upon the volume of legislation in which an agency or department is involved, may consume a substantial part of the time of a top-level legal officer, and in some organizations, may require

[11] A. B. Wildavsky, *The Politics of the Budgetary Process* (Boston: Little, Brown & Co., 1964), pp. 83 and 85.

equal or greater efforts on the part of other highly trained lawyers in the immediate office of the General Counsel.

Fifth, many or most agencies employ a congressional liaison officer to handle still other, or to oversee all, relations with the Congress. The activities of these staff men (and women) range from the handling of large volumes of congressional correspondence to the resolving of delicate and substantive issues that arise between the Congress and the agency or department. They may focus on dealings with two or more committees and whatever tasks are required to assure kindly consideration by those committees of bills that are especially important to the agency. Suffice it to say that in December, 1964, President Johnson commented in an official release that he regarded the role of the congressional liaison officer as second in importance only to that of the head of the agency![12]

The five channels through which many (or most) congressional-departmental relationships flow do not comprehend all contacts between the Hill and the Executive Branch. The contacts are numerous, their purposes diverse, and the range of individuals involved within the bureaucracy is broad. Indeed, the relationships with the Hill are so numerous and frequent, and so often consequential, that it is unrealistic to picture them only in terms of the budget officer, the personnel director, or the congressional liaison officer—or only as an activity which the program manager would perform personally if his time permitted. Congressional relationships make a continuous claim on the time of the supporting staff managers, particularly of the budget director and the congressional liaison officer.

Responsibility to Constituencies

The successful program manager, it was pointed out in Chapter II, is continually aware of and attentive to the interest

---

[12] Of the forty-six men and women identified earlier as congressional liaison officers (see footnote 1 on page 55), half had been active in Democratic party affairs prior to undertaking their current assignment, virtually all were between thirty and fifty years of age, one-third were career civil servants prior to assignments to this role, and some were outstanding experts in their fields (e.g., P. P. Claxton of the Department of State in mutual security affairs).

groups that are especially concerned with the work of his agency. What similar responsibilities do *supporting staff managers* have to these interest groups or to other constituencies?

For those supporting staff managers whose roles are defined not in terms of a particular function, but by their relationships with their bosses,[13] the constituencies are synonymous with those that confront the program manager. Indeed, these "general purpose" assistants frequently serve as the liaison with groups outside the agency. For example:

> The Deputy for Supply and Maintenance in the Air Force represents the Secretary's office at meetings of important service and industry groups such as the Air Force Association, the Aerospace Industries Association, and the National Security Industrial Association.
>
> The Special Assistant for Community and Congressional Relations in the Civil Aeronautics Board acts as the intermediary between local communities and their representatives in Congress and the air carriers in an attempt to prevent "fires" in the air transport field before they start. One such fire required a meeting with the officials of Lancaster, Pennsylvania, and their Congressmen who were anxious to retain airline service to Lancaster. Meetings of this type and speeches before similar groups require an estimated "fifty-man-days per year" of this official's time.

For the majority of supporting staff managers—i.e., those responsible for a function—the interest group or constituency they relate to is more commonly an agency of the federal government that oversees the function (e.g., personnel—the United States Civil Service Commission, legal—the Justice Department). It is from these special constituencies that the functional specialist expects criticism and looks for guidance, approval, and support. To make the point more explicit, let us illustrate the more common constituency relationships of the supporting staff managers. The budget officer has his ties and allegiances to the Bureau of the Budget and the relevant subcommittee of the House Appropriations Committee. The personnel man continually deals with and has ties to the Civil

---

[13] I.e., deputies with broad management responsibilities throughout the agency, and assistants-to whose activities involve personal assistance to the program manager or special-project-type assignments.

Service Commission. The finance or accounting man is regularly in touch with and attentive to the General Accounting Office (GAO) and to a lesser degree the Treasury. The procurement specialist is expected to follow the lead of the General Services Administration. The security officer has less official but often important relationships with the Federal Bureau of Investigation (FBI) or the Central Intelligence Agency (CIA) and occasionally with special congressional investigating committees. The congressional liaison officer serves not only as the channel of communication with the Congress, but sometimes as the voice of a particular congressional committee or its chairman.

The supporting staff manager appraises the program manager's demands in terms of the standards and opinions of the relevant functional control agency.

DISTINCTIVE CHARACTERISTICS OF
THE STAFF MANAGER'S ROLE

The preceding pages offer a firsthand view of what supporting staff managers actually do, in place of the usual meaningless generalizations about "staff" services. Yet generalization is needed. We must distinguish carefully between supporting staff managers and those other upper-level career people we classify as program managers and professionals.

1. *The supporting staff manager possesses and utilizes knowledge gained from experience in a specialized field of public management.*

Two-thirds of the supporting staff managers have spent their entire federal service in the same occupational field. In contrast, half of the program managers have concentrated in the occupational field in which they are now employed. Those with two or more areas of specialization had had this experience, in most instances, in another occupational field within the first years of their working career.

Consider, for example, the careers of ten accountant-comptrollers. Seven spent their entire working careers (averaging 16.3 years) in accounting-comptrollership activities. Two entered the field after eight and nine years of service respectively in other fields; since then they have devoted themselves, for twenty and twelve years respectively, continually to accounting work. The career of only one man offers an exception. After twenty-one years of service—including five in general administration and fifteen in personnel administration—this individual assumed his current position as comptroller of a 17,000-man agency.

Similarly, only two of ten personnel officers included in this group had held jobs outside the field of personnel administration after the first five years of their service in the federal government. Only one worked outside this specialized field for more than five years out of the twenty or more years each man has served.

A different kind of specialization is apparent in the careers of congressional liaison officers. Of eleven identified earlier, who held this post in either civilian or military agencies,[14] most have had long experience in their present organizations (an average of 16.7 years) and still longer experience in the Executive Branch (22.9 years). Some of these have worked as liaison officers in two or more agencies. One took four years out from his career service to work as administrative assistant to a Senator.

Specialization in a function is apparent even among the assistants-to. A majority of these men reached their present jobs after proving their worth as a specialist in personnel, in budgeting, or in another managerial support field. Indeed, four of every five men classified as assistants-to reported that all their experience had been in a single occupational field.

The staff manager, however, appears better able than his colleagues in program or professional positions to carry his specialized experience with him from agency to agency. A personnel officer in the Internal Revenue Service previously practiced personnel in the Department of Agriculture and the Securities and Exchange Commission. And a comptroller in the Commerce Department gained earlier comptrollership

[14] See footnote 12 on page 68.

experience in the General Accounting Office and the Department of Interior. In fact, almost half (49 per cent) of the staff managers in this study have worked in three or more bureaus throughout their federal careers, as opposed to less than one-third of the program managers and slightly more than one-fifth of the professionals.

2. *The staff manager in the federal agency is not accurately described as an extension of the executive himself; most staff managers direct substantial staffs that provide generally required services.*

Traditional management thinking from the time of Frederick W. Taylor's introduction of the staff concept in 1911 has pictured the staff specialist as an extension of the executive himself. Recent observers of management recognize the limitations of this early idea. For example, John Pfiffner and Frank Sherwood have written:

> The traditional concept of staff is aid to the executive. This is presumably to be done without disturbing the formal command relationships in the hierarchy. Yet increasing specialization in the organization and growing pressures on the top executive have complicated this initially simple concept greatly . . .
>
> Today it is more useful on many occasions to think in terms of two types of activity within the organization: (a) that which is *substantive* (direct) in its contribution to the organization's over-all objectives, and (b) that which is *adjective* (indirect) in its contribution. Such a way of thinking removes some confusion and permits us to define staff in somewhat different terms. Staff should be thought of as a *process* occurring around the executive. This process involves thinking, planning, and organizing.[15]

Few functional staff managers described relationships with the boss in picturing their activities. One who did, identified his boss as one of several to whom he was responsible; his duties entailed working with "the Administrator, the Associate Administrators, and several other deputy administrators."

[15] *Administrative Organization*, by John M. Pfiffner and Frank P. Sherwood, Professors of Public Administration, University of Southern California (Englewood Cliffs, N.J.: Prentice-Hall, Inc., © 1960), p. 171. See also Gerald G. Fisch, "Line-Staff is Obsolete," in *Harvard Business Review*, September-October, 1961, pp. 67–77, who gives a similar but supplementary explanation of the obsolescence of the line and staff concept; and see O. Glenn Stahl's article entitled, "The Network of Authority" in the Winter, 1958 issue of the *Public Administration Review*.

The words of some (e.g., budget directors, personnel officers, procurement specialists) indicate that they acknowledge a responsibility to the program manager (i.e., the executive) but are quick to point out that, in fact, their staffs exist to provide a service that is needed by all or most divisions of the agency. One personnel director typified perhaps an extreme example of these multiple allegiances:

> The nature of my position requires that I be accessible, at any and all times, to practically any individual, official, or employee, who may wish to confer with me. I must be available for inquiries from members of Congress, officials of the Office of the Secretary . . . as well as those contacts from within my own organization and even within those areas which I control, i.e., my Assistant Director, branch chiefs and their subordinates. I make every attempt to stop what I am doing and to consider the problems which they bring to me as they present themselves in my office or arrange to meet with me.

A Finance Officer in the Public Health Service pictured in similar terms this same obligation to all who require the service for which he is responsible. His work, he said, is "subject to adjustment or cancellation because of urgent demands from congressional committees, officials in the Office of the Secretary, representatives of the Bureau of the Budget, or higher officials in the Public Health Service."

The supporting staff manager, as a provider of specialized services to many in the agency, has a relatively substantial staff to aid in providing this service. Of 105 managerial specialists in this study, nearly 15 per cent had staffs of 500 or more. The Director of the Procurement Division in the Post Office Department's Bureau of Facilities, for example, directs a staff of 1,500 people in the development of policies and regulations, and the supervising of procurement in the 587,000-man department.

Perhaps one vestige of staff that *is* an extension of the executive comprises those assistants-to whose duties are deeply involved with communications skills. For example, an assistant for congressional affairs or for press relations often works closely with his boss, and is identified with and speaks for him. These close and continuing relationships give weight to the argument that the assistant-to is an extension of the executive. But even in such instances, the assistant-to may be (and sometimes is) more a *rival* to than an extension of the executive.[16]

3. *The staff manager in a federal agency "represents" a government-wide function.*

Within the federal service, central control agencies establish standards and maintain surveillance over the performance of each specialized staff function (e.g., personnel administration, budgeting, accounting, procurement) in every agency and department. The Civil Service Commission, for example, is the center of authority and policy leadership in personnel administration throughout the Executive Branch. The Commission:

—reviews agency recruitment and classification practices;
—develops work measurement and cost analysis techniques for personnel activities;
—allocates supergrade positions throughout federal services;
—speaks to the Chief Executive and to the Congress on all matters involving personnel administration, e.g., federal pay legislation;
—conducts personnel investigations (some 40,000 in Fiscal Year 1962) of prospective federal employees.

These actions set for the departmental, service, or bureau personnel director a code of personnel practice. He is expected to represent his agency, contribute to the development of service-wide policies, and enforce the policies prescribed by the Civil Service Commission. In day-to-day operations, he frequently interprets the Commission's policies as a dictate from superior authority. Similarly, the budget officer relays and interprets the views of the Bureau of the Budget, and the finance officer the views of the General Accounting Office.

4. *The staff manager performs a function that is in part a control upon the program manager.*

---

[16] Whistler, *op. cit.*, notes that a requirement of a successful assistant-to is that he be able and willing to work entirely for his boss. But he points out that the strong-minded assistant-to often begins to think more and more of the opportunities his position provides for his own personal progress.

Supporting staff managers exercise several kinds of control:

—the personnel officer, in recruiting employees or classifying positions, controls people and positions according to the way in which he interprets standards set by the Civil Service Commission;

—the budget officer controls when he approves or disapproves budget requests in line with what he thinks the Bureau of the Budget will allow, or in accordance with discussions with the staff members of the Bureau or of the appropriations committee;

—the fiscal officer prescribes rules and procedures for his agency according to his views of what the General Accounting Office—the government's accounting watchdog—will approve; and

—the procurement specialist buys for the organizations in his agency in terms of standards and guidelines set by the General Services Administration.

The *supporting staff manager* is looked to for advice regarding the probable position of the agency on whose views and rulings he is expert (e.g., the Civil Service Commission or a relevant congressional committee). Hence, some tend to assume a position of control. They "advise" that this or that action will not be accepted or approved by the agency whose views they represent. An authority on personnel describes this control function in these words:

Each supervisor is his own personnel man and budget man—up to a point. That there is such a point is important. Some conditions must be established organization-wide which set boundaries on supervisory decision-making . . . [The supporting staff managers] . . . inevitably become the interpreters and, to a considerable extent, the real enforcers of these limits.[17]

But the problem is that not all supporting staff managers are in agreement as to the ends of management. Some contend that the "how" is as important as the "what":

It is idle to rationalize all of our organization structure and behavior on the theory that sustaining management activities are invariably and forever subordinate to the initial program objectives of the organization, particularly when it is a governmental organization . . . [18]

[17] "More on the Network of Authority," by O. Glenn Stahl, *Public Administration Review*, Vol. 20, No. 1, Winter, 1960, p. 36. "The thing to be guarded against is the attitude that program administration is always paramount and that there is no such thing as a proper *method* of doing it—such as sound personnel operations—*as an end in itself.*" *Ibid.*, p. 37. Reprinted by permission of the American Society for Public Administration.

[18] *Ibid.*, p. 37.

For good or ill, the advice that is imposed by the supporting staff manager, in the name of his functional foster parent, tends to split the task of decision-making. Authority for decisions that significantly influence the program manager's ability to get the job done is denied him.

Chapter IV

THE PROFESSIONAL AT THE TOP OF THE FEDERAL SERVICE

THREE OF EVERY TEN individuals who serve in the upper levels of the federal career service practice a profession. Their number includes physical scientists, life scientists, physicians, social scientists, actuaries, engineers, and lawyers.[1]

Individuals with some of these skills, performing similar roles, were found in the federal service more than a century ago.[2] But their number, roles, and status have changed markedly since World War II. Rapid technological advance has ex-

[1] Wallace S. Sayre in "Scientists and American Science Policy," *Science*, Vol. 133, © March 24, 1961, p. 862, has pointed out that "the life scientists . . . occupy many special units in Agriculture, in Health, Education, and Welfare, and in Interior; the nuclear scientists are found in the Atomic Energy Commission, and other physicists and chemists, in the Bureau of Standards; meteorologists staff the Weather Bureau; scientists of many varieties inhabit Defense Department units; while the geologists have their sanctuary in the Geological Survey, the space scientists have theirs in the National Aeronautics and Space Administration, and the economists have theirs in the Council of Economic Advisers. The other social sciences are less visibly accommodated, but they do staff numerous units in Agriculture, in Commerce, in Health, Education, and Welfare, and in Labor." Copyright 1961 by the American Association for the Advancement of Science.

[2] Frances L. Williams in "Mathew Fontaine Maury," *Scientists of the Sea* (New Brunswick, N.J.: Rutgers University Press, 1963), describes the activities in the 1830's of the Superintendent of the Naval Observatory, the Secretary of the Smithsonian Institution, and the Superintendent of the Coast Survey.

panded the place of the scientist and the engineer. Enactment of the Employment Act of 1946 has generated new responsibilities for economists. And the evolution of the processes of administrative law in a government of vastly expanded functions has created the need for thousands of lawyers, most of them highly specialized in patent law, in food and drug legislation, in labor law, and in still other fields.

Previous studies of the upper levels of the federal career service have tended to lump these professionals together with all other civil servants of like rank in the analyses they have offered.[3] While these authors have recognized some differences in the role played by "scientists," the professionals have customarily been classified as "executives" along with program managers and supporting staff managers. And it has been concluded that the responsibilities of all these individuals are similar or identical, that they can be (or are) recruited in the same manner, that their development and training logically follow the same course, and that the means of motivating and utilizing other top-level career civil servants is equally applicable to the professionals.

This chapter holds those assumptions up to the light. It describes how and with whom these professionals spend their time. It analyzes the kinds and the breadth of responsibilities they have. And it identifies the distinctive capacities required in men who have risen to the highest level of the career service in these fields.

THE WORK OF TYPICAL PROFESSIONALS

The stereotype of the federal executive seldom includes the scientist experimenting in the laboratory, the doctor heading a service in a large hospital, the economist analyzing current indices of the nation's economic health, the engineer working to stem the rising tide of water pollution, or the lawyer drafting a brief or new legislation. The stereotype implies that the

[3] David and Pollock, *op. cit.* See also Warner *et al.*, *op. cit.*, although here there was recognition of the non-executive role of physicians and some other upper-level civil servants. And finally, the Stanley study, *op. cit.*

management tasks of the director of a research laboratory, or the chief economist who supervises the work of a group of economists, or the general counsel responsible for the work of a score of lawyers are similar or identical with those of the program manager and the supporting staff manager. And this stereotype allows for no distinction between the executive who runs a field organization of 15,000 clerical and administrative employees performing relatively routine tasks and the executive who is a psychiatrist and who spends a part of his time on research with patients even while he counsels with a dozen or more less experienced psychiatrists who are working on their own projects.

To identify this group—the *professionals*—that makes up a significant portion of all upper-level civil servants, we present here brief sketches of the work of selected professionals in the federal career service.

Dr. Lloyd A. Wood is Director of the Air Force's Physical Science Division in the Office of Scientific Research. Dr. Wood, with a twenty-two-man staff, was responsible for a budget of $13 million in 1964. Most of this sum goes to finance basic research in the physical sciences carried on through research grants and contracts to universities, institutes, and industrial laboratories throughout the country. In more than twelve years of federal service, Dr. Wood has worked as a research chemist and a branch chief in chemistry research. He has pursued research in his chosen professional field—aeronautical and space research—in positions in both the Air Force and the National Aeronautics and Space Administration.

Dr. Harlow W. Ades, a Ph.D. in zoology, is Head of the Navy's Neurological Sciences Division in the Naval School of Aviation Medicine. He and his fifteen-man staff do research in the neurophysiology of hearing and the effects of noise on the inner ear. Their work involves such tasks as supervising the Navy's Hearing Conservation Program and related research for the Bureau of Naval Weapons, directing the evaluation of aviation helmets and communications gear, and acting as consultants to the Bureau of Medicine and Surgery, other Defense Department agencies, and universities.

William V. Crosswhite is the Internal Revenue Service's Regional Counsel in the New York City Region. He and his 115-man staff advise district directors of Internal Revenue on questions arising out of the collection of taxes. They represent the service in cases before the Tax Court and prepare criminal actions arising under the Internal Revenue laws for prosecution through the Department of Justice.

Dr. Haskell P. Wald directs the 25-member Office of the Federal Power Commission. Dr. Wald and 15 professional economists and statisticians in his office submit evidence in rate and certificate cases and provide the five Commissioners with research studies and policy analyses to aid them in reaching decisions.

Each of these professionals heads a unit specializing in the application of a particular discipline to the work of their agencies. Thus, their day-by-day activities involve some executive duties similar to those of the supporting staff manager, e.g., Mr. Crosswhite. Other professionals carry on activities that are less similar. They may be described as *performers;* they work alone or with little staff to assist them, contributing a specialized experience, training, and acknowledged expertise to the work of the agency they serve. Here are some typical examples.

Dr. Norman A. Haskell is a Senior Scientist in the Air Force's Cambridge Research Laboratories. A Ph.D. in geology, Dr. Haskell, with the assistance of a nine-member staff, personally conducts research in earth physics and theoretical seismology. In addition, Dr. Haskell initiates and administers research contracts with a number of universities and industrial research organizations in the field of seismology.

Dr. David W. Bluestone, a Ph.D. in economics, is Director of the Civil Aeronautics Board's Planning Office. With a three-man staff, he advises the five Board members on "strategic planning" of major substantive Board policies and programs and helps to establish over-all Board objectives. He brings to the deliberations of the Board the results of continual economic analysis of the future problem areas in air transportation.

Dr. Lawrence E. Chermak is legal officer to the Comptroller of the Navy. Dr. Chermak advises on all fiscal-legal questions relating to the Department's $15 billion annual budget in matters of financing, disbursing, auditing, accounting, and contracting. He possesses unique competence in business administration and in law that equips him for this particular assignment. He was engaged in the private practice of law before he commenced upon eighteen years of public service.

This chapter pictures, through the words and activities of the individuals themselves, the roles and responsibilities of a growing number of top-level career civil servants who play an essential role in the functioning of the federal government.

THE PROFESSIONAL IN TOP MANAGEMENT

About two-thirds of the 1,200 "professionals" found in top-level career positions in 1963 were employed in the fields of law, research (physical and medical), and the social sciences—particularly economics—and were responsible for the production of staffs of professionals engaged in work on specialized problems. The remaining third, whom we have classified as "performers," operated alone or with very few staff members to assist them. Nearly half of the entire 1,200 worked in the Defense Department. Other pertinent characteristics that distinguish this group from among all upper-level civil servants are indicated in Table 3.

In what respects, if at all, do the tasks and responsibilities of these lawyers, scientists, and economists differ from those of the program manager? Or of supporting staff managers? Are these professionals removed by the disciplines of their professions from the task of getting the job done? Are their responsibilities narrower in scope and different in kind? Are they "involved" in the program as distinguished from their profession? Do they accept responsibility for achieving program objectives in the same measure as do program managers?

Modern management doctrine tends to picture the professional as one who descends periodically from his pinnacle of

Table 3. A Profile of the Professionals Compared with All
Upper-Level Civil Servants*

	Pro- fessionals	All Upper-Level Civil Servants
Average age	51.9	52.0
Marital status	98% Married	96% Married
Education: *Per cent* of college graduates with at least one advanced degree	76.2	60.1
Field of study: *Per cent* listing law, economics, or engi- neering	50.0	43.6
Entry into federal service: *Per cent* entering prior to 1940	40.8	50.9
Length of federal service: *Per cent* with more than twenty years	51.5	59.9
Starting grade: *Per cent* starting at GS-7 or below . .	47.7	54.7
Attained supergrade: *Years* required	15.4	16.7
Number of bureaus worked in: *Per cent* working in no more than two	77.6	66.6

Service outside the government: *Per cent* who have
   worked outside the federal government since date of
   entry . . . .
	15.4	14.9

Concentration in occupational field: *Per cent* who re-
   port all jobs since entry into federal service have been
   in same occupational field . . . .
	80.8	76.2

* See Appendix B for a more complete summary of these findings.

professional wisdom to invent a new and more terrifying
secret weapon, adjudicate a complex legal impasse, prescribe
how a higher level of economic well-being will be achieved,
or guide the uninformed administrator. Is this concept of the
role of the professional confirmed by analysis of his day-by-day
activities?

The end product of the professional's work in most instances takes one of two forms: (1) a completed project, as for
example a report on an experiment or on the design of a piece
of equipment, prepared either by him and his staff or by a
contractor or grantee whose work he has financed; or (2)
advice given in one of a variety of ways to a superior or to
others. How are such projects and advice related to the pro-

gram of the agency with which the professional is associated?

Robert J. Myers's contribution to the conduct and evolution of this country's social security program offers an illustration. Mr. Myers entered the federal service as a "junior actuary" in 1934. Gradually he advanced until in 1947 he was promoted to the post of Chief Actuary of the Social Security Administration.

He and his staff (a total of about fifteen professionally trained actuaries) are engaged, at any particular moment, in a series of analyses of operating data to forecast the probable cost of each significant element of the social security program. These projects may originate in amendments to the social security laws introduced in the Congress, such as that lowering the retirement age for men from sixty-five to sixty-two. They often originate with administrative and policy-making officials who require data as to prospective costs in developing operating plans or in formulating new social security programs, Medicare being a case in point. Or they may be studies designed to aid the Advisory Council on Social Security to evaluate operations under existing law.

Myers's completed projects are often "cost estimates," i.e., the cost in terms of aggregate benefits that must be financed if the social security laws are amended in a particular way. His cost estimates do not encompass the whole range of issues the Commissioner of Social Security and the Secretary of Health, Education, and Welfare, or the Congress, or the Advisory Council take into account, but his estimates are unusually influential. They bear—and Myers's word bears—an authority that grows out of an acknowledged expertness demonstrated repeatedly over a quarter of a century.

Or take the example of Dr. David Shakow, Chief of the Laboratory of Psychology of the National Institute of Mental Health (NIMH). He heads a staff distributed among six sections, each of which is engaged in psychological research that together is planned to reveal new understanding of mental illness. The completed project is usually a bit of new knowledge or the further development of a scientist in this field. Responsibility for ensuring the relevance of those "end-products" to the broad and often quite general objectives of the parent agency rests on Dr. Shakow's shoulders; but this responsibility must be discharged in terms of the Institute's commitments to basic research in those substantive areas for which it is responsible.[4]

Or consider a specific project completed by the Chief Economist of the Federal Trade Commission and the action that resulted:

> "This matter" [a proposal for undertaking a particular economic-legal approach to an important area of the Commission's work], he wrote, had been the subject of discussion over a period of several months. Beginning Monday afternoon, I began work on a memorandum detailing the approach to be followed. I received staff assistance on facts, etc. This memorandum was finally completed by me Saturday morning, typed Monday morning, distributed to interested parties, and the suggested course of action was accepted at a conference held with the affected legal bureau Tuesday afternoon.

> "This project will involve the work of about five lawyers and five economists over the next year, and expenditures of about $100,000. It will constitute one of the major programs of our economic divisions during the next year. It involved a combination of performance, planning, and coordinating activities. I worked closely in the development of this matter because it was a subject with which I was intimately familiar."

The task of advising takes on numerous forms; illustrations of this variety indicate how and to what extent the professional's effort is related to, and the manner in which he is responsible for, achieving the program objectives of the agency with which he is associated.

An assistant general counsel in the Department of Health, Education, and Welfare *advised*, by drafting a letter of opinion to a White House staff member, the extent to which the Public Health Service was authorized to grant funds for public narcotic addiction prevention programs.

[4] An excellent description of the setting within which the professional carries on his work within the federal service is found in Delia and Ferdinand Kuhn, Editors, *Adventures in Public Service* (New York: Vanguard Press, 1963), Chapter 6, "Out of the Snake Pit." This chapter describes the career and the work of Dr. Robert H. Felix, formerly Director of the National Institute of Mental Health. The contrast of the responsibilities of Dr. Felix, pictured there, and the responsibilities of his subordinate, Dr. Shakow, illuminates the range of responsibilities of the program manager and those of the professional.

In other instances—many other instances for those professionals employed in the Defense Department—advising takes the form of briefings, i.e., the preparing and presenting of materials that inform their superiors. For example,

> A technical director wrote of a meeting in which "three hours and fifteen minutes were spent with the director, commander, project manager . . . and the Bureau's program and project managers . . . to show the Bureau all was being done to try to ensure success in . . . flight tests. This meeting was occasioned by the fact that the past five flight tests have been unsuccessful and people in the [Secretary's Office] wanted assurance that steps were being taken by the Bureau people. The Bureau people knew what was being done, but needed to say they had reviewed it all with the director and commander, and that they knew the top management of this laboratory was aware of and approved the steps being taken."

Similarly, the Scientific Director of the Quartermaster Food and Container Institute was asked to report on a crash program to supply special indigeneous forces with lightweight, flexibly-packed, native foods. He spent more than fifteen hours in Washington and in the Institute's Massachusetts laboratories, preparing a briefing for the Secretary of Defense and for officials of the Advanced Research Projects Agency. The actual presentation of the report took but one hour.

These "briefings" may involve verbal reports or they may involve more elaborate presentations requiring extensive preparations, supporting materials, rehearsals, and several "live performances."

On occasion, professionals resent time consumed by these briefings. An Air Force scientist explained his resentment in these words:

> The information transfer rate in briefings seldom exceeds 120 words per minute. My reading rate is about 360 words per minute. Hence, reading has a three to one advantage over oral briefings which advantage should be increased by the factor of verbosity of speakers.

To sum up, the professional, like the program manager, is held responsible for: (a) accomplishing certain stipulated objectives, (b) advising his superior on specific aspects of the total program, (c) assuring the competence and effectiveness of the staff used to accomplish these ends, (d) providing essential administrative services, and (e) maintaining harmonious relations with other agencies involved in the program. The objectives the professional is expected to accomplish are limited in scope; they are *not* coterminous with the responsibilities of the program manager. Rather they are limited to the reach of the particular discipline the professional practices. The professional's responsibility for providing advice is similarly limited, even though it may be influential (or controlling) in any specific area. In succeeding pages, other responsibilities of the professional will be contrasted with those of his colleagues at the upper levels of the federal service.

Responsibility to Superior

But to what extent do the activities of the professional indicate that he occupies a distinctive position within the organizational hierarchy? Does his responsibility to his superior differ from that of other individuals of like rank within the organizations?

In relation to his superior, the professional typically demands and is granted relatively greater freedom in determining *how* he shall carry on the work in which he is expert—even *what* work he shall carry on—than is the program manager or supporting staff manager.

   The Technical Director of the Navy Electronics Laboratory in San Diego, for example, met—during the week for which his activities were studied—with his Associate Technical Directors to plan a major part of the Laboratory's research and exploratory development program, described as the independent program. This portion of the Laboratory's total program is defined and planned by the Technical Director and his Associates with technical proposals coming from the entire technical staff. No subsequent review is made by superiors other than final approval by the Commanding Officer and Director of the Laboratory and the *post facto* examination of results by the Office of the Assistant Secretary of the Navy (R&D) and by the parent organization, the Bureau of Ships.

   Or consider the freedom enjoyed by the Research Seismologist of the Coast and Geodetic Survey (C&GS). He spends approximately a third of his time advising his colleagues in the C&GS, and others in government. The balance of his time he devotes to such research as *he* deems most fruitful in light of over-all C&GS objectives, and in counseling his two technical assistants to whom he extends similar freedom.

Yet, the professional finds it necessary—and desirable—to keep his superior informed of the things that are going on in his area. He does this through more or less continuous exchanges of information. He must be sensitive to his boss's needs and seek to learn the depth to which his superior wants to be informed. For upon this activity may depend the superior's acceptance of the professional's advice and the superior's support of the professional's efforts and staff. On many occasions, the superior seeks such information.

The Chief of the Federal Trade Commission's Division of Scientific Opinions, for example, was asked to show how his professional employees were being utilized and to explain why certain projects were delayed. Such administrative requirements dispel any illusion that the scientist, the economist, or the lawyer is wholly set apart within the hierarchy because of his expertise.

Another example: the Director of the Defense Supply Agency requested that Counsel bring him up to date. Specifically, he wanted to know what steps had been taken to protect stored household goods of military personnel, the manner in which fraud cases were being handled by a field installation, and what was the extent of his (the Director's) responsibility for negotiated sales of firearms to state and municipal agencies.

The time and effort spent "informing" depends on the superior and on the relationships between him and his professional subordinate. In the aggregate, for the sample of 130 professionals, the time and effort devoted to keeping the boss informed was minimal. But in the Department of Defense, where most agencies are headed by a military officer subject to periodic transfer, the time required is greater. The career civilian professional, as the Number Two man, periodically has to orient new superiors to the job. The technical director of one research facility voiced this complaint (implicit in the words of others) that he has had to "break in a new C.O." every two years or less. Most of these superiors, he added, "had never been in R & D work" and started out intending "to run a taut ship"; it takes time to establish a satisfactory working relationship.

While the professional demands, and usually is given, large freedom to plan his own and his staff's efforts, he is called upon periodically to explain and defend his program and his accomplishments.

Responsibility to and for Subordinates

Except for the so-called performers, who work alone or with a very small staff, professionals bear a large responsibility to their staffs. Yet this responsibility differs from that borne by the program manager or the supporting staff manager. The program manager's activities cut across many functions, often comprehend numerous organizational sub-divisions, and include a variety of supporting specialists. In contrast, the professional is responsible for a smaller organization, a narrower function, and a more homogeneous staff. On the average, the professional supervises less than a fourth of the employees supervised by the program manager, and slightly more than half of those supervised by the supporting staff manager. And, on the average, he spends less time supervising or attending to staff needs than do either the program manager or the supporting staff manager.

The activities of representative professionals reveal that their supervision of subordinates has two distinctive characteristics:

(1) it is focused, in major part, on substantive issues; and (2) it is carried out, in the words of one professional, with "a very loose rein."

The Director of the Internal Revenue Service's Research Division reported that about 35 per cent of his time is spent working with subordinates on economic-tax questions.

"To provide the needed guidance, coordination, and control," he wrote, "it is necessary that I be reasonably well acquainted with all technical aspects of the projects underway. This does not mean that I need be the 'best' statistician or 'best' economist, or 'best' in any particular discipline; rather, it means that I should have the most comprehensive understanding of the way in which all pieces of work fit together, and a decent degree of competence in the various disciplines. A balanced, critical sensitivity is always much in need; likewise, a background of experience with respect to the most effective approach to take in 'selling ideas' to other officials of the Service."

Despite this official's disclaimer of expertise, the professional's staff looks to him for guidance of a sort that requires understanding that is both broad and deep. The experience of a division head at the Navy's Pacific Missile Range illustrates this point. He spent three hours with three members of his staff "at their initiation," hearing opposing technical viewpoints on a study in which they were involved. His ability to gain agreement among the trio as to the future course of the study and to give specific directions rested on their acceptance of his professional judgment and their confidence in his objectivity.

Whether he is a scientist, an actuary, an economist, or a lawyer, the professional believes that the best use of his (and of his staff's) talents and experience will be achieved if he and they are given wide latitude in determining what work to perform and how. That this precept is generally accepted in practice is illustrated by the comments of the chief of one of the National Bureau of Standards' scientific sections. This official, a chemist, regards each of his seven-man staff as "independently working scientists." Each pursues tasks which follow from his own particular area of specialization, yet fit into the objectives of the section. The chief of the section visualizes his own role as that of "planning ahead, giving advice to each member of his staff, reviewing the work being done, and handling budget problems."

A further comment touches on a distinctive aspect of the professional's responsibility to his staff. To maintain a "very loose rein" and thus to motivate the professional subordinate to apply his expertise and initiative, the professional—in practice—continually takes the lead in seeing to it that resources are available, in developing individual staff members, and in "selling" their proposals and accomplishments.

In day-by-day operations, this means that upper-level professionals devote from 10 to 20 per cent of their time to such activities as these:

—*Planning and Representing.* A division director in the Navy's Bureau of Ships spent more than half his time, during the week surveyed, developing a budget for forty-five projects. He then presented plans for those projects and the budget for the approval of his immediate superior and commanding officer. After selling them, he prepared written material to transmit their recommendation of his program to the Admiral in charge of BuShips.

—*Supervising.* An Associate Technical Director of the Naval Ordnance Laboratory at White Oak, Maryland, spent much of the week (during which his activities were under the spotlight of this study) resolving a jurisdictional dispute that shackled the effort of a technical group for which he is responsible. He sought the details from the technician in charge and presented the facts to his immediate superior. This matter was then summarized in a memorandum which the Chief of the Bureau of Weapons used as a basis for discussions with the Chief of Naval Operations.

—*Obtaining and Retaining Personnel.* The Technical Director of an Army research installation at White Sands Missile Range met with one of his electronic engineers who had received an offer from an industrial group to help him establish his own electronics business. The employee had come in to seek opinion and advice on the future of the Army's research activities in his area in view of the continuing reorganizations within the department. The director gave the employee "a frank appraisal of his future" within the Army organization. Later, in discussing the meeting, he noted, "I consider the obtaining and retention of technically competent personnel one of the most important functions of my position."

What a bureau director in the Department of Health, Education, and Welfare described as a "crisis" affords still a fourth illustration of the upper-level professional's responsibility to his staff:

The crisis was created by the disapproval of requests for travel to foreign meetings by the Office of the Secretary (HEW), after such requests had always been approved over a period of years. "Ordinarily, I spend less than one hour weekly on the consideration of foreign meeting travel requests. But to placate the 1,600 professional and scientific personnel in this bureau, I had to draft a protest and then obtain a hearing with the Secretary. This consumed a lot of time—that I needed for more important work."

Irritation over the approval of travel is typical of the administrative "tight rein" against which professionals often rebel. They complain that such controls consume time they should be spending on professional work. One regarded the review of scientific positions (required by the personnel officer) as "a waste of time." Another complained of the time required to review a letter drafted by the Office of Personnel to a Senator who had intervened on behalf of a field employee who had been fired. Still another professional complained of the requirement that he make out officer fitness reports: "[I] do not regard this type of report as relevant to the functions of a scientific research organization."

In summary, the responsibility of the upper-level professional to and for a staff (most of them trained in the same discipline in which he—the boss—was trained) is effectively outlined by a report prepared within the Department of the Navy. In essence, that report concluded that it is ridiculous to think that people who handle laboratories, or R & D, or systems development can do so effectively without an appreciation of the scientific mode of approach or of modern engineering.[5] The report further made clear that the professional who directs a staff of professionals must be capable of maintaining an organization within which needed administrative services are readily available, and capable of helping his staff to understand and accept the rules governing their application. In short, all organizations made up wholly or largely of professional men and women possess unique characteristics that must be understood if the fundamentals of management are to be applied effectively.

Responsibility to the Profession

Analysis of the professional's responsibility to his superiors, for his staff, and to the objectives of his agency indicates that to succeed, the professional must command from his staff, his colleagues, and his superiors (and often from the public) respect for his professional capacities. The maintenance of such respect and the furtherance of his reputation as a chemist, a

[5] Report (and subsidiary departmental reports) of the Research and Development Task Group of the Study of Management Education and Training Programs within the Department of Defense, January, 1963.

psychiatrist, a rocket specialist, or a tax lawyer requires persistent diligence. To a greater extent than the program manager or the supporting staff manager, the professional is expected to (and does) seek to preserve, develop, and expand his professional competence. He does this in several ways.

First, he devotes a significant portion of his time (during and after working hours) to keeping up—reading and studying in his field or doing personal research. It is difficult to determine what proportion of such efforts is required by his position and what is the result of his dedication to the discipline. For some at least, professional commitment is obvious. The Superintendent of the United States Naval Research Laboratory's Solid State Division explained that he strives to devote from 30 to 50 per cent of his time to personal research.

This activity, he declares, "is important because it broadens one's background, permits stimulation of personnel, freshens one's appreciation and understanding of the problems of science and, of course, gives one a sense of accomplishment through recognition of the work."

Most professionals have to sandwich such efforts between other competing tasks. The Chief of IRS Technical Planning Division's Corporation Income Tax Branch, for example, keeps up with developments in the tax field by reading at home the leading cases, selected articles in tax journals and law reviews, and even the digests and summaries of decisions by other IRS personnel. But a few, most of them the performers, devote major portions of their time to expanding their professional lore. The Senior Scientist of the Aerospace Research Laboratories reported that he spent a third of his time in "the conduct of personal research in gravitational and electromagnetic physics."

Most professionals rely on the evening hours to maintain their professional skills and knowledge. Data collected on their expenditures of time indicate that they spend more time than either the program managers or supporting staff managers, doing their "homework." On the average, the program managers reportedly worked 4.2 overtime hours, the supporting staff managers 3.1, and the professionals 4.8 hours.

Second, the professional keeps up by exchanging views with the best men in the field. For many, this is inherent in their work. A technical director for research management in the Air Force Aeronautical Systems Division, for example, met with scientists from the Georgia Institute of Technology to discuss their possible participation in an Air Force research project. The director of an Army laboratory invited a top-flight group of industrial executives, nongovernmental scientists, and others to help solve a particular space research problem with which he was confronted. Similarly, the senior civilian scientific advisor in Army Intelligence met with his counterpart in the British Defense Department to discuss the use of digital computers in intelligence activities.

A further part of the professional's continuing job involves participation in professional meetings. The Head of the Navy's Neurological Sciences Division spends an estimated seventy-five to eighty days a year attending and traveling to national and international scientific meetings.

A common method by which many federal agencies obtain the views of professionals outside the government is the advisory council. For the professional in government (who often sits with the council or acts as its executive secretary), the advisory council is an added and sometimes invaluable forum for the exchange of ideas, for keeping abreast of advance in the profession, and for becoming known to leaders in the field. Moreover, his participation in the making of significant decisions on problems of national importance, and often the resources (e.g., dollars, facilities, and people) he can marshal in the solution of these problems, gives to the professional in government a distinction in his field of great value to many.

Third, many recognize a responsibility for contributing to the development of thought in their professions. Many write and publish, speak to professional groups, and accept the obligation to respond to inquiries about their work.

The Chief Statistician of the Bureau of Naval Weapons, for example, spent six hours over a weekend and two hours in his office preparing a technical paper on a new advance in sampling techniques incorporated into the American-British-Canadian sampling standards. This paper was to be presented at an international management congress.

The Chief of the Air Force Logistics Command's Operations Analysis Office met with superiors, peers, and subordinates in preparation for the writing of a speech to be delivered to a world-wide Operations Analysis Conference. The speech was finally written by him during the course of his summer vacation.

An occupational health scientist in the Public Health Service spent twenty-five hours writing scientific papers on thermophysiology—"to communicate [the] results of thoughts, compilations, and research results to scientific colleagues."

A chief scientist in the Agricultural Research Service estimated that he spends about an hour each day answering questions about plants and soils posed in correspondence generated by his previous publications. "A large part of this correspondence," he reported, "deals with the review of manuscripts for scientific journals."

The fact that the well qualified professional is a reservoir of expert knowledge and is available to other professionals or to the public is sometimes burdensome. For example, a Forest Service research director spent an hour reviewing a paper "as a courtesy to a fellow scientist." Also as a courtesy, the Associate Technical Director for Underseas Technology in the Navy's Bureau of Ships met with visitors from half a dozen different companies for a total of more than six hours during a single week. But courtesy ran out when a director of one of the technical divisions in the Navy's Bureau of Medicine and Surgery was visited by a retired Navy commander and an engineer from a private firm:

These individuals consumed one hour of my time and that of the physicist in my division. They represent a large group of semi-nomadic itinerant amateurs of science who, operating on generous contracts from government agencies, go about visiting working laboratories trying to get ideas for working out programs for their own projects. These are usually people who have a computer of sorts or a similar fashionable gimmick and are trying desperately to find something to do with it that will serve to ensure a contract renewal for a higher rate for the next year. They are time-wasters who are just barely well enough accredited by some Department of Defense agency to make it advisable for us to see them, at least, briefly, instead of setting the dogs on them at the door, as they deserve.

The obligations of the professional to his colleagues elsewhere in the agency, in other federal agencies, or outside the government arise naturally out of his position in the agency, his professional standing, and his accessibility as a reachable, recognizable civil servant. The effect is substantially to enlarge the range and number of professional contacts he enjoys, even while it burdens the individual with many extra demands upon his time.

Responsibility to Constituencies

It is perhaps difficult to visualize the key scientist, departmental counsel, actuary, or economist involved in the pulling, tugging, persuading, and negotiating with Executive agencies, the Congress, and constituent groups as a necessary part of getting the job done. Yet analysis of what they do indicates that professionals are involved in these concerns.

Frequently, professionals are called upon to meet, assist, or entertain those who for one reason or another are important to the parent agency and its programs. For example:

> The Associate Director for Research of a large Naval laboratory had to deal with a company scientist who, this professional reported, was "actually a salesman interested in marketing his company's product."
> The Director of the Forest Products and Engineering Research Division in the Forest Service met with a team of industrial consultants to discuss the technical aspects of possible pulping processes to produce corrugated board from hardwoods.
> The General Counsel of the Export-Import Bank conferred with the Counsel of the Foreign Credit Insurance Association, a New York association composed of about 72 insurance companies, who, with the Bank, had been drawn into a lawsuit in the state courts of Tennessee. They discussed a memorandum supporting a petition to remove the case from the state to the federal court.

Sometimes professionals are called upon to defend or to drum up support for their agency's programs with powerful, nongovernmental groups.[6] The Director of Transportation

---

[6] "The Bureau of Mines must listen attentively to the American Mining Congress and the United Mine Workers; the Bureau of Standards to many industry associations; the Weather Bureau to the Air Transport Association and the Farm Bureau Federation; the Public Health Service to the American Medical Association and the American Cancer Society; the National Aeronautics and Space Administration to the aviation industry associations (and often to committees of the National Academy of Sciences); the Atomic Energy Commission to the electric power associations and

Research in the Post Office Department, for example, develops and maintains analyses as to passenger train scheduling that help to counter charges of the American Association of Railroads that the Post Office Department is ruining the railroads by taking the mail off.

On more occasions, the professional participates in positive efforts to gain support. For example, the Economic Advisor to the Secretary of Agriculture lunched with the president of the powerful National Wheat Growers Association to gain support for proposals designed to benefit the growers.

The extent of such contact with important constituencies varies markedly among departments and individuals. Scientists and engineers in most agencies meet regularly with their counterparts in private contractor companies and also with professionals from companies that are considered as potential contractors to their agencies. They appear before contractors' associations and technical committees of these associations. Similarly, lawyers, economists, and actuaries often meet with their opposite numbers in organizations with which their agencies are legally, contractually, or financially involved.

Congress and its committees represent, for the professional, an especially important advisee. The lawyers frequently are involved in negotiating for their organizations on legislation or in adding support to requests for added authorization. But scientists, economists, and other professionals are frequently called upon to appear before and to advise substantive and fiscal committees.

Consider these typical examples of dealings on the Hill by professionals:

> The General Counsel of the Export-Import Bank met with staffs of the House and Senate Banking Committees to attempt to work out a compromise on a bill which would extend the life of the Bank for an additional five years.

---

many contractor groups; and agricultural research bureaus to the Cotton Council and numerous other commodity associations. Rare is the science bureau which is not required by its political environment to bargain continuously with and accommodate its aims and its priorities to the interest groups in its constituency." Wallace S. Sayre, "Scientists and American Policy," *Science*, Vol. 133, © March 24, 1961, p. 862. Copyright by the American Association for the Advancement of Science.

The Chief of a large weapons project in the Department of Defense testified before the Senate Appropriations Committee to justify the transfer of $1.1 million from the Defense budget to the Commerce Department budget, after the House Committee had omitted this item in their passage of the Fiscal 1964 Appropriations Bill.

The Deputy Grants Policy Officer of the Public Health Service prepared a paper concerning grants to medical schools. The paper and subsequent discussions of it were initiated by the Clerk of the House Appropriations Subcommittee on Labor and HEW, a critical committee in terms of the Service's continued financing.

The technical advisor of the Air Force's Arnold Engineering Development Center is responsible for representing his organization before the Air Force Headquarters, the Department of Defense, and the Congress. He presents and justifies the need for technical facilities for the Center. Last year, these representations required approximately forty days of his time.

Generally, those in highly technical and scientific fields tend to avoid appearances on the Hill. Some, such as the technical advisor referred to above, are directed to represent their organizations before the Congress. Others appear willing to go only when the continuity or growth of their programs is at stake or when their individual expertise has a peculiar relevance to the deliberations. This reticence is attributable, on the one hand, to the fact that the scientist feels that many Congressmen do not speak his language, and on the other hand, to the willingness of these professionals to have the program manager and his administrative assistants discuss general policy matters or appropriations.[7]

DISTINCTIVE ASPECTS OF THE ROLE
OF TOP-LEVEL PROFESSIONALS

The activities of the professional in a federal bureau, office, or service are essential to the functioning of the organization and are an integral part of it. But at the same time, the role of

[7] On those occasions when substantive committees of Congress call representatives of the scientific and technical communities to testify on scientific or technical questions directly related to their work, there is little apparent reluctance to appear. Such inquiries by Congress are fairly common incident to questions as to aerospace technology, atomic energy, weapons development, or the future of the economy.

the professional and his organizational status is clearly distinguishable from that of the program manager or of the supporting staff manager. To begin with, the professional is less concerned with problems of *command*. He spends perhaps a fifth
less time than the program manager on matters of direction,
control, and staffing. And he spends less time than either
the program manager or the supporting staff managers in
persuading others to his point of view—in negotiating, representing, and coordinating. He is much more involved in *performing;* nearly 30 per cent of his time is spent doing the work
himself. And he spends appreciably more time *alone* (about
seventeen hours a week) than his colleagues. These quantitative measures suggest respects in which the professional differs
from the program and supporting staff managers; they do
not reflect more subtle aspects of his work.

These characteristics are suggested by the following six
generalizations as to the role and status of the professional in
the federal service.

1. *The career professional who serves in an upper-level position is
first a scientist, a lawyer, a doctor, an actuary, or an economist and
second a division or bureau chief.*

The professional's activities in government are marked by
the relatively large proportion of his time that goes into the
formulation and the giving of advice. To be effective in this
role and to discharge his related responsibilities, he must
possess a substantial and specialized understanding of the
discipline he represents and he must command the respect of
his staff, his colleagues, and his superiors for his effective application of that discipline. A consequence of this concentration is
an allegiance to the discipline which at the least vies with, and
sometimes challenges, his allegiance to the division or bureau
he serves.[8]

2. *The professional expects—and is expected—to devote a substantial
portion of his time and energy to developing, maintaining, and expanding his professional capacity.*

The requirements for continually reading, studying, reviewing, and writing to develop professional competence and to

[8] Sayre, *op. cit.*, pp. 859–64.

demonstrate this competence are apparent in the activities of professionals in this study. On the whole, the doctor, the scientist, the engineer, the economist, or the lawyer spends more time working alone—studying, performing research, writing technical papers, and reviewing similarly weighty manuscripts —than does either the program or supporting staff manager.

The motivation is mixed. The professional must maintain his competence in a field of specialization in order to serve the division or bureau of which he is a part. And his personal advancement lies in most instances within his profession or discipline more than in the governmental agency of which he is a part. For many professionals there is no "step up" within the hierarchy; the top job is reserved for a nonprofessional. Advance lies in enhancing his reputation in the profession.

3. *The professional occupies a relatively independent status within the organizational hierarchy.*

Traditional organizational theory holds that responsibility and authority are delegated vertically downward in an organization. It holds, too, that such responsibility and authority may always be withdrawn by the superior.[9]

That theory was spelled out long before the degree of specialized expertise that now exists had become apparent. There are responsibility and authority that the General Counsel, the Chief Economist, or the Medical Director derives by virtue of his expertise that are not delegated and cannot be withdrawn.[10] Some would contend that the responsibility and authority of these professionals are analogous to the expertise of the supporting staff manager who serves as personnel director, as finance director, or as procurement officer. The analogy fails, however, when one considers the extent to which the program manager usually is obliged to accept the recommendation of the aide in each of these fields; he usually will not

[9] For realistic consideration of such theory, see Bertram Gross, *The Managing of Organizations* (Riverside, N.J.: Free Press of Glencoe, 1965), Vol. 1, pp. 308–10.

[10] This same independent status is observable in the careers of some supporting staff managers who have developed their special expertise (e.g., "getting along with the commission," or "selling the budget on the Hill"). But the likelihood of its appearance is somewhat greater in the more esoteric areas of science, law, and economics.

hesitate to substitute his own judgment in making decisions in the fields of personnel, finance, and procurement, even while he respects the recommendations of his aides. However, he seldom will substitute his own judgment for the recommendation of the professional in the fields of science, law, medicine, actuarial science, and economics.[11]

The program manager may complain (and often does) of the arrogance of the professional, of the insistence by the lawyer, the economist, the actuary, the doctor, or the scientist that the precepts of his discipline permit only one course of action. But in the end, the program manager takes a contrary course with substantial risk.

4. *Yet, the professional is by personal choice and by function integrally associated with the agency's programs and objectives.*

The professional is employed by the governmental agency to apply his discipline to the problems of the agency. The marine biologist who serves on the staff of the Under Secretary of State is there to bring his expertise to bear on the international problems of commercial fisheries. The economists who serve on the staffs of the Department of Justice and the Federal Trade Commission have the pragmatic task of applying their lore to the cases these agencies handle. The lawyers in scores of agencies bear the continual and heavy burden of "keeping the boss out of trouble"—i.e., of showing him how he can achieve program objectives within the letter of the law, and of drafting the language and formulating the persuasive arguments required to win congressional support for proposed legislation.

[11] This point is eloquently illustrated by an editorial comment of *The New York Times* on July 25, 1965 ("The News of the Week in Review," p. 2E). *The Times* wrote: "The accounts published last week [accounts of the Bay of Pigs incident by Arthur Schlesinger, Jr., and Theodore Sorensen] showed that before the invasion Mr. Kennedy, despite all his self-confidence and poise—stood unduly in awe of the military and C.I.A. experts. 'If someone comes in to tell me this or that about the minimum wage bill, I have no hesitation in overruling them,' Mr. Schlesinger quoted the President as telling him. 'But you always assume that the military and intelligence people have some secret skill not available to ordinary mortals' " (© 1965 by The New York Times Company; reprinted by permission). So it often is with the program manager and his professional associate—the actuary, biologist, chemist, engineer, physicist, and others.

Only a small minority of the physical or life scientists that serve the government are engaged in basic research that has little or no immediate application to the agency's current program and objectives. The bulk of the physicists, chemists, astronomers, and others perform functions integrally a part of the agency's effort to accomplish objectives. For example, the astronomer on the staff of NASA will be immediately applying her knowledge to the development of the orbiting astronomical observatory or inducing other astronomers in the universities to collaborate on the development of this experiment.

5. *The professional's activities require that he be capable of communicating his knowledge effectively and defending it persuasively both inside and outside the agency.*

This point was put well by the Director of the Internal Revenue Service's Research Division when he described several meetings with counterparts of other divisions in the Service:

> Since the Research Division is basically an idea factory, one important test of the fruitfulness of our efforts is the success we have in convincing other branches of the Service of the soundness of the views and recommendations that we put forth. This is idea selling in the best sense of the term.

Of all activities reported by the professionals studied, those consuming a major portion of their time, perhaps three-fourths, can be described as group activities. The professionals were involved in conferences, meetings, and discussions with subordinates, peers, superiors, and people from outside the agency and the federal establishment. Many individuals with whom the professional comes in contact—among his colleagues, in the Executive Office, and in the Congress—do not speak the same language. They depend (and the professional's own success depends) upon his ability to translate complex ideas into understandable terms. It is in this latter context (i.e., difference in language) that the professional's need to communicate and to defend differs from that of the program manager and supporting staff manager. His discipline is enshrouded, to a greater degree than the personnel man's or the budget officer's, in the specialized languages of microbionics, macroeconomics, mathematics, or the law. He must translate abstruse concepts into the everyday language of members of Congress, of his constituencies, and of those around him so that they will understand and be convinced. His task of communication is often a more difficult one and, unfortunately, one for which many professionals are less well prepared than are the program and supporting staff managers.

6. *Two-thirds of the professionals who serve at the topmost levels of the federal service must, in addition to possessing skill in their discipline, manifest a capacity for managing others in the same or related disciplines.*

One observer recently commented on the professional's regard for management:

> By and large, the scientist sees the manager as a bureaucrat, paper shuffler, and parasite; a noncreative, unoriginal hack who serves as an obstacle in the way of creative people trying to do a job, and a person more interested in dollars and power than in knowledge and innovation.[12]

The intolerance indicated by this statement reflects as much a failure on the part of general administrators to understand the unique aspects of managing professional workers as it does the intolerance of the professional with essential administrative routines. Decisions as to staffing, planning, budgeting, and supervising the work of professional people revolve around an understanding of the issues involved. These decisions command respect by those affected only when they are made with an appreciation and understanding of the issues and comprehension of the processes of orderly administration.

The professional's possession of an understanding of the issues is not enough. He must understand the nature and logic of administrative processes and be capable of applying these processes with a full appreciation of the motivations of professional workers.

[12] Harvey Sherman in a speech before the American Society for Public Administration, National Capital Area Chapter, September 23, 1964.

Chapter V

THE SUMMING UP:
WHAT THEY DO AND
HOW THEY ARRIVED

No SINGLE PROFILE of those at the top of the career service can provide an adequate basis for evaluating the work experience of the more than 5,000 individuals who occupy these positions. For these men and women at the top differ in the nature of the tasks they perform. As the preceding three chapters have shown, some manage large programs through huge field staffs, others provide essential supporting services in a host of functional fields, and still others are repositories of expert knowledge and advice in scientific, economic, or legal matters.

There are still further differences. These men and women manage and support programs in more than a hundred different federal agencies. These programs, in turn, encompass an even broader array of activities from building ships to coining money, from developing biological warfare agents to providing financial support to the needy. At first glance, one might conclude that the only thing which the Director of Travel Promotion of the United States Travel Service and the Senior Scientist for Aerospace Research in the Air Force have in common is that they are paid by Uncle Sam!

On reflection, however, there appear to be truly significant generalizations that can be drawn concerning the three principal groups identified in this study. These more significant differences relate to the differing character of the responsibilities borne by those men and women who fill the top career program, supporting, and professional posts. The responsibilities borne by individuals in each group differ in four crucial respects:

—*In the Ultimacy of the Responsibility.* The program manager, in the final analysis, is responsible for accomplishing the program—for producing results. And either his hierarchial superior—the Secretary—or a congressional committee looks to him for that accomplishment. The supporting staff manager and the professional are responsible for contributing to the program, but their responsibility falls short of the program manager's. Often their contributions are not visible or measurable, though their influence may be great. And it is the program manager who—if he is doing his job—must appraise and accept or reject their efforts.

—*In the Source of Authority and the Focus of Responsibility.* The program manager derives his authority from the Secretary (or agency head) who looks to him as the motivating force for the program (though some managers certainly derive authority and power from the congressional committee). The supporting staff manager, on the other hand, derives a major portion of his authority from the central functional agency and is responsible to that agency, even if in a less direct fashion. And the professional's authority stems, in large part, from the expertise he possesses as a member of a profession. He is responsible to his peers in the profession, even while answerable to the program manager.

—*In the Extent to Which Authority Is Subject to Challenge.* The program manager, in accounting for his responsibility, is challengeable by the congressional committee, or earlier by the Secretary, on the basis of political or public policy. His response to these challenges depends on his relations with the Secretary and the committee, the importance and visibility of his program, and the prevailing political climate.

The supporting staff manager is challengeable because his expertise—in personnel or budgeting—is seldom the only or final determinant in management decisions. The program manager may readily substitute his judgment for that of the personnel man or the budget officer especially if he regards himself as equipped in the ways of the bureaucracy with respect to these functions. But he will less often substitute his judgment for that of the lawyer or the scientist whose expertise tends to be even more specialized and less related to the experience of the program manager. In some considerable part, the program manager's willingness to challenge the judgments of his supporting specialists is proportionate to his comprehension of their disciplines.

—*In the Nature and Breadth of the Span of Control.* The manager of a large program is responsible for a variety of specialists whose skills he must interrelate, and whose contributions he must comprehend. These specialists include those on his own staff, the number and composition of which will change as the program alters in size and character; and they include the part-time services of managerial specialists and professional advisors who serve him and other program managers.

In contrast, the supporting staff manager or the professional usually supervises only other specialists in his own field. As a physicist, economist, or personnel officer, the staff manager or professional shares a common disciplinary interest with those he supervises; this common interest is normally unavailable to the program manager.

There are then discernable differences in the ways that individual program managers, supporting staff managers, and professionals react to the responsibilities they bear. These differences arise in part from the different paths followed by individuals in each group on the way to the top. As Chapters VI and VII will show, there are important distinctions in the ways those in each group should be recruited, developed, and promoted to these upper positions.

Before appraising the steps required to ensure the continued quality of the federal government's top career management, it might be well to look at the career patterns of those who now occupy top program, support, and professional positions. For to the extent that these patterns do *not* yield the experience and ability required in the future, they represent opportunities for improvement.

ASCENT OF THE CAREER LADDER

How did the men whose activities have been pictured in the three preceding chapters rise to the positions of eminence they now occupy? Did their preparatory educations and their work careers equip them for the responsibilities that they now carry? In what respects do the preparatory educations and work careers of program managers, supporting staff managers, and the professionals differ?

Many of the career civil servants who occupy supergrade positions, probably a majority, reached their present posts after an experience such as this. The new entrant entered the federal service well before age thirty with an advanced degree. He came in at grade GS-7[1] and at the end of five years reached grade GS-11. By the ten-year mark, he had attained grade GS-13, but he did not make supergrade until he had put in nearly seventeen years in the career service.

The work experience which he brings to his present job and which now exceeds twenty years was acquired largely within the federal service—and within the department by which he is now employed![2] Prior to entering the federal service, he had had only incidental work experience—summer jobs, and perhaps a year or more in private business. After entering, he worked in only one or two separate departments; if he has worked in more than two, he probably switched jobs before age thirty and then settled down to a career within a department. And his total experience in federal service has been—in the main—within a single occupational field.[3]

---

[1] Of the respondents 54.7 per cent entered at grade GS-7 or below.

[2] Fifty-nine point nine per cent have more than twenty years of service and 14.4 per cent have more than thirty years of service.

[3] The picture of the typical supergrade that emerges from this study is not unlike that drawn by other studies of the same group.

In short, the breadth of experience, the skills he has acquired, and the breadth of understanding he brings to his present assignment have all been developed on the job within the federal service. This practice is analogous to the experience of individuals found in large private enterprises. But the question remains: Does that experience develop the capabilities required for the positions that have been pictured in the preceding chapters?

The answer to this question is of prime importance to the effectiveness of these civil servants who influence very substantially the quality of the services provided by the several departments and agencies that make up the federal government. Two factors are important in seeking answers to the question. The first relates to the periods of entry of these men and women into federal service. The second pertains to the radical changes that have occurred and are occurring in the manager's job.

1. *Most of those at the top of the career service today were selected in a buyers' market.* The bulk of the 5,000 came into federal service at one of two relatively unique periods. In the 1930's, government employment offered many a challenge and an opportunity to solve new and big problems. For others, graduated out of college and into the depression, government was the only employer interested in their services and willing to pay.

Later, during World War II, the career service was swelled by an additional influx of workers.[4] The workforce was flooded

---

Stanley's study, *op. cit.*, pp. 33–34, for example, which included people at grade GS-15 as well as the supergrades, shows a slightly younger employee (age fifty). Yet his findings with respect to occupational and organizational mobility are strikingly similar.

The Warner study, *op. cit*, pp. 167–68, indicates considerably greater mobility among its survey respondents, but this appears to be the result of two factors: (1) the study includes people at lower grade levels (down through grade GS-14), and (2) the design of the question relating to organizational mobility not only makes no allowances for the difference between long and very short tenure in various agencies, but also treats the departments of Army, Navy, and Air Force as well as the Office of the Secretary of Defense as separate organizations.

[4] For example, civilian employment in the Executive Branch of the federal government nearly tripled in the years 1940–1944 to reach a peak of more than 2.9 million in July, 1944.

by war workers, and later with returning veterans eager to resume lives long broken by war and in need of jobs. Once again, government service offered opportunity and, through the rapid passage of veterans' preference laws, somewhat favored treatment.

Since these two periods, there has been no comparable wave of public enthusiasm. After Russia's Sputnik orbited the world in 1957, there was some improvement in public appreciation of the opportunities for interesting and stimulating work in government. President Kennedy added further attraction to federal service by the new programs he created and the "tone" he set. During the years since 1957, there have been evidences that some people are eager to come in, particularly to a few "glamor" agencies, even at a financial sacrifice. All in all, however, the picture painted by many has been dim. [5] The prevailing image of the federal civil servant in the minds of most citizens has been that of a lackluster individual doing relatively routine clerical or administrative work in unimaginative fashion. There has been an unfortunate and widespread misunderstanding of the work that top-level civil servants do.

The inaccurate but common picture of federal employment as less demanding and more routine than industry has discouraged many of the more aggressive and achievement-minded people from even considering the possibilities of federal employment. The apparent differences between the periods of the 1930's and 1940's and succeeding years have caused many to question whether the quality of top management can be sustained in the future.

2. *The tasks of managing programs and providing managerial and professional support are increasingly more complex and difficult now than they were only 20 years ago.* There are several reasons for this:

> —The goals of government are increasingly more numerous and involved. The concepts of health, education, and welfare have been broadened to include programs and functions considered impossible two decades ago.

[5] Kilpatrick, *et al., op. cit.*

—The degree of specialization has increased. The basic disciplines of physics, chemistry, and biology are split and joined in new fields such as bionics, astrophysics, and microelectronics.

—There are many more kinds of specialists whose work must be managed and coordinated. Many foreign aid teams, for example, include scientists and technicians in education, agriculture, engineering, credit and banking, municipal government, and industrial development.

—The constituencies with which the line manager and the supporting managerial and professional staffs must be concerned are more vociferous and powerful. Top-career servants face special interest groups and competing agencies that are better fortified and armed than ever.

—The management tools available are ever more sophisticated, efficient, and expensive. Complex computers and esoteric techniques (e.g., operations research, systems management, mathematical programming) must be understood and properly applied by the manager to solve his problems.

—And finally, with the apparent escalation at the upper levels of the Civil Service grade structure and in the face of growing budgets for many programs, there has been an increased emphasis—within the federal government—on personnel and budgetary controls.

Thus, the processes that produce top managers and supporting specialists to meet these more complex and difficult tasks must result in even higher levels of excellence than before, but without the favorable recruitment conditions that prevailed when most of those at the top came in.

If the vital processes by which individuals are selected, experienced, and developed (or trained) for these posts at the topmost levels of the federal career service are to be improved, appraisal must precede change. To that end, the following pages summarily depict, for each of the three functional groups, the educational experience and work careers that have brought these individuals to their present positions.

EQUIPMENT AT ENTRY

When today's upper-level career servants began their federal careers, they brought with them certain basic qualifications of age and education and, on the basis of these qualifications, were assigned rungs in the career ladder. But the equipment brought by these individuals to their first jobs varied, sometimes significantly.

—*Age at Entry.* Six out of ten of the present supergrades began their federal careers before they were thirty. Some started even earlier; nearly 40 per cent of the program and supporting staff managers came in at or before age twenty-five. In contrast, only slightly more than one quarter of the professionals were in federal service at age twenty-five. For the most part, the professionals joined later—nearly two-thirds between their twenty-sixth and fortieth birthdays (as compared with about half for the program and supporting staff managers). Relatively few (11 to 12 per cent) came in after age forty.

Table 4. Age at Entry into Federal Service

Group	Up to 25 yrs.	26–30 yrs.	31–40 yrs.	Over 40 yrs.
Program Managers	39.5%	19.7%	30.0%	10.8%
Supporting Staff Managers	38.8	25.2	24.5	11.5
Professionals	24.6	30.0	33.8	11.6

—*Education.* By any reasonable standard, the men and women at the top of the career service are well educated, better educated, by and large, than their counterparts in private business.[6] Ninety per cent have college degrees. Sixty per cent have an advanced degree.[7] But, of the degree holders, three out of ten earned their highest degrees *after* they entered

Table 5. Education at Entry into Federal Service

Group	Non-degree	Baccalaureate degree	Baccalaureate plus one or more advanced degrees
Program Managers	23.2%	76.8%	31.9%
Supporting Staff Managers	25.9	74.1	25.1
Professionals	6.9	93.1	46.9

[6] Warner, *op. cit.*, pp. 113–14.

[7] One-fifth were educated in law, 17 per cent in biology or the physical sciences, 13 per cent in engineering, 9 per cent in economics, and a smattering in other fields such as accounting (6 per cent), business administration (3 per cent), or public administration (3 per cent).

federal service.[8] Still, as Table 5 shows, these individuals entered federal service with good educational backgrounds.[9]

These educational differences among the three managerial groups are marked. Not surprisingly, the professionals were the most highly educated with the fewest "non-degree" people and the most advanced-degree holders. The older age and higher education brought by the professionals reflect the correspondingly higher entrance qualifications. For the professional—the doctor, scientist, economist, or lawyer—is required to bring a body of knowledge and an outside qualification (e.g., an M.D. degree or a law license) to his job.

—*Entry Grade.* The benefits of these higher qualifications are apparent in Table 6 which shows starting grades of the three groups. The program and supporting managers came in at lower levels than did the professionals; fewer lateralled in at the higher grades (GS-10 and up). Thus, the program and staff managers began younger and were less well educated, and developed their special skills on the job.

Table 6. Starting Grades in Federal Service

Group	Less than GS-4	GS-4 through -9	GS-10 and higher
Program Managers	16.4%	50.2%	33.4%
Supporting Staff Managers	24.5	38.1	37.4
Professionals	8.5	48.5	43.0

[8] The following percentages of each group reported that their highest degree was attained "after entrance into federal service": program managers, 32.8; supporting staff managers, 29.1; and professionals, 27.1 (corrected to eliminate those who entered federal service without degrees).

[9] Available evidence indicates that the situation which prevailed at the time most of these people came in has changed substantially. Under the Civil Service Commission's "Quality Graduate Program," a significant proportion of those brought into federal service is better qualified than were today's supergrades on their entry into federal service. For example, of 14,671 individuals appointed to the first two professional career grades (GS-5 and 7) during the period January 1963 to June 1964, approximately one-fifth were "quality" graduates, i.e., they entered federal service on the basis of superior college records, honor society membership, high scholastic averages (B+) in major subjects, etc. See "Report on Use of Quality Graduate Standards," U.S. Civil Service Commission, March, 1965.

RAPIDITY OF ASCENT

Progress in the federal service, as elsewhere, is seldom uniform. Some individuals with higher educations or sharper intellects, or who possess special skills in great demand, or who became associated with rapidly expanding agencies, outdistance their peers in the race to the top. Judged simply on the basis of the number of years of service required to achieve supergrade, the professionals appear to have done better (15.4 years) than either the program managers (17.8 years) or the staff managers (16.9 years). Generally, the professionals were more mature and better educated when they came in and were thus able to command higher starting salaries.

A better view of the progress of each group is provided by three comparisons of the rapidity of their ascent in relation to the grades at which they entered federal service.

1. Table 7 compares the progress of program managers, staff managers, and professionals who entered the federal service at grade GS-4 or below. In this case, a larger percentage of the professionals reached supergrade earlier. Their edge began to show ten to fifteen years out, and by twenty years, nearly twice as great a proportion of professionals "made it" than did program or staff managers.

Table 7. Proportions of Each Managerial Group Entering Federal Service at Grade GS-4 and under, Who Attained Selected Grades after Prescribed Periods of Service

Group	*Number* entering at GS-4 and under	*Per cent* who attained GS-11 or higher by 10 years*	*Per cent* who attained GS-15 or higher by 15 years*	*Per cent* who attained supergrade at 20 years or earlier
Program Managers	32	53.1	6.3	18.8
Supporting Staff Managers .	41	80.5	7.3	15.0
Professionals	13	61.6	30.8	30.8

* Includes those who attained these grades *before* they had been in service for the prescribed period.

2. Table 8 similarly compares those in each group who entered the federal service at grades GS-5 through -9. This table indicates that those program managers who entered federal service at grades GS-5 through -9 did fairly well early in their careers, but increasingly less well in later years. For those in this category (which includes the principal starting grades for today's college graduates, GS-5, -7, and -9), both the professionals and supporting staffs did better than the program managers. In light of the program manager's heavy and primary responsibility for program objectives, as described earlier, it is curious that he should be the last to reach the top.

Table 8. Proportions of Each Managerial Group Entering Federal Service at Grade GS-5 through -9, Who Attained Selected Grades after Prescribed Periods of Service.

Group	Number entering at GS-5 through -9	Per cent who attained GS-11 or higher by 10 years*	Per cent who attained GS-15 or higher by 15 years*	Per cent who attained supergrade at 20 years or earlier
Program Managers	66	89.5	36.4	33.3
Supporting Staff Managers .	51	94.2	56.9	61.0
Professionals	61	93.5	50.9	57.5

* Includes those who attained these grades *before* they had been in service for the prescribed period.

The explanation lies partly in a characteristic of expanding organizations; as organizations grow (in private enterprise as well as in government), there is a tendency to expand the number of staff positions, while the number of line positions grows more slowly. In short, the opportunities for program managers have been fewer than those afforded staff managers and professionals. The program manager's relatively slower rate of progress may also be attributable to the fact that he is less mobile, being characterized by a substantial commitment to a single program. Therefore, the program manager has fewer opportunities, for example, than the supporting staff manager, whose expertise is more likely transferable from one agency to another.

3. Finally, Table 9 compares the progress of those who entered federal service at grades GS-10 or higher. Thus, even those who "lateralled in" to higher supporting and professional positions moved faster than entrants to similarly graded program spots. On the whole the program manager's progress, at whatever level he came into federal service, appears slower than that of the staff manager and the professional.

Table 9. Proportions of Each Managerial Group Entering Federal Service at Grades GS-10 and Higher, Who Attained Selected Grades after Prescribed Periods of Service.*

Group	Number entering at GS-10 and higher	Per cent who attained GS-15 or higher by 10 years**	Per cent who attained supergrade at 15 years or earlier
Program Managers	49	67.3	71.4
Supporting Staff Managers	55	81.8	83.6
Professionals	56	80.5	85.8

* Note different column heads in this table.

** Includes those who attained these grades *before* they had been in service for the prescribed period.

If we look at those who lateralled in at an even higher level, say GS-13 and above, the results are not so signficant as to distinguish them from their peers who have come up through the ranks. They are only slightly younger (51.2 years as opposed to 52.0 for the entire sample), average out to the same grade (GS-17), and are not significantly better educated. The picture presented in this area is not sufficiently precise to allow generalization with respect to the quality, adequacy, or detailed characteristics of the lateral entrants as a whole.

Still another view of the rapidity with which those at the top reached their positions is gained by singling out those who attained supergrade either significantly faster or slower than their colleagues. Those in this study have been divided into (a) 10 per cent (forty-two respondents) who achieved supergrade *faster* than their colleagues—usually by their thirty-sixth birthday, (b) 10 per cent who achieved *slower*—usually by age fifty-nine, and (c) the remaining 80 per cent who—on the average—reach supergrade by about their forty-eighth birth-day.[10] As Table 10 shows, those in the youngest group had less total federal service, fewer years between their entry date and their attainment of supergrade, and reached supergrade at younger ages than their colleagues.

Table 10. Years of Service and Average Age at Supergrade

	Youngest group	Oldest group	Middle group
Average total *years* of service	8.3	26.3	21.5
Average *years* of service to supergrade	6.5	20.3	17.9
Average *age* at attainment of supergrade* . .	36.2	58.8	48.1

* Edward McCrensky in an unpublished "Study of Career of Federal Personnel Holding Key Positions at GS-15 and Above," supplies supplementary and generally confirmatory data. Of the sample of 232 individuals McCrensky studied, for those who achieved grade GS-15 in fifteen years or less, the average age at attainment was 43; for those who achieved grade GS-15 in twenty years or less the average age was 46; and for those who achieved grade GS-15 in "over twenty years," the average age was 50.

A relatively high percentage of the youngest (27 per cent) began their careers in the supergrades, a figure much higher than either the oldest or middle groups (11.9 and 4.1 per cent respectively). Most likely, this reflects the bringing in of lateral entrants who possess needed and special skills not available within the bureaucracy.

Generally speaking, those in the youngest group are the best educated. As Table 11 shows, they lead significantly in both basic and advanced degrees.

Table 11. Education of the Three Groups

	Youngest group	Oldest group	Middle group
Per cent with at least a baccalaureate	97.6	83.3	91.4
Per cent with one or more advanced degrees . .	77.7	64.3	50.8

[10] Analysis of these three groups is based on an unpublished paper prepared by Marty R. Rockway, a career civil servant of the Department of the Air Force, during a year spent at Princeton University. Using the survey questionnaires, Mr. Rockway divided survey respondents according to their ages at attainment of supergrade.

There is no evidence to indicate that the youngest have been penalized because of their youth. Comparison of the current grade levels of those in the three groups (Table 12) shows that the youngest group has the highest percentage of grade GS-18's and certainly a respectable portion of the 17's and 16's.

Table 12. Distribution by Grade Level

Grade	Youngest group	Oldest group	Middle group
GS-16	47.6%	45.2%	52.3%
GS-17	16.7	26.2	20.6
GS-18	7.1	4.8	5.9
PL 313-III	11.9	2.4	4.7
PL 313-II	9.5	11.9	10.0
PL 313-I	7.1	9.5	6.5

These data suggest that those who rise rapidly and those who come in as lateral entrants are superior individuals, at least as measured by educational achievement. Some have done remarkably well in their relatively short careers, achieving supergrade within seven years at under forty years of age. Most of these fast movers seem to be concentrated in two fields: general administration and the physical sciences. And they include slightly more supporting staff managers and professionals than program managers. In contrast, program managers account for 50 per cent of the oldest group, and they make up a sizable portion (31 per cent) of the youngest group.

The rapid achievers, then, appear to be those who have been brought in at relatively high levels (40 per cent came in at GS-13 or higher), or—entering at lower levels with better than average educational backgrounds and usually (though not always) in supporting positions—who have ambitiously and aggressively striven for advance and arrived sooner than their peers.

RANGE OF CAREER EXPERIENCE

Organizational Mobility. Most of the men and women at the upper levels of the career service are relatively inexperienced in agencies and occupations outside those in which they are now employed. Nearly half (47.4 per cent) are in the same agencies and 39.2 per cent are in the same bureaus in which they began their careers. For seven out of ten, all their jobs in the career service have been in a single occupational group.

A substantial proportion of each of the three groups had a tendency to stay put in the organizations where first employed, as shown in Table 13. While more of the supporting staff managers moved, over half worked in no more than two bureaus throughout their entire careers. Professionals, the least mobile, include a higher proportion who came in at higher levels (more than one-fifth at grade GS-13 or higher) and who had less total service.

Table 13. Number of Different Bureaus Worked in Throughout Entire Career in Federal Service

| | Number of Bureaus | | |
Group	One	Two	Three or more
Program Managers	45.6%	26.5%	27.9%
Supporting Staff Managers	25.8	25.2	49.0
Professionals	46.9	30.8	22.3

Movement among Occupations. There is equally limited movement among occupational fields. Roughly three-fourths of the program and staff managers and four-fifths of the professionals reported they were still working in the same fields in which they began their careers. Even among those who had moved, many shifts were accomplished relatively early in their working lives. Indeed, as Rufus Miles has effectively pointed out, the federal civil service system effectively binds the individual to a career in a "narrow classification series or occupational field."[11]

[11] "Mobility, Stability, and Sterility," by Rufus E. Miles, Jr., *Public Administration Review*, Vol. 23, No. 3, September, 1963, pp. 199–200. "Once a young man or woman with first-class ability is placed on one of the various position series escalators, the chances are he will move up rapidly to a grade-level where he can no longer consider broadening his experience and usefulness by transferring to another position series. To do so, he would have to step back one or more grades. The most he can hope for as a means of gaining breadth of perspective is to be given the opportunity for participation in a training program ranging from a week or two to a school year." Reprinted by permission of the American Society for Public Administration.

Table 14 shows occupational changes reported by program managers, staff managers, and professionals, grouped according to three periods in which they occurred. Two kinds of changes are shown in the table. "Fundamental changes" are those in which an employee shifted from one occupational field to another and stayed there. "Independent excursions" are those relatively brief tours outside the occupation for purposes such as military service, private business, or service in an international organization such as the United Nations, when such tours did not directly relate to the respondent's occupational specialty.

Table 14. *Numbers of Changes* in Occupation Reported by Ninety-nine Respondents According to Three Separate Periods in Which They Occurred

	Periods			
	Up to 10 years	11–20 years	Over 20 years	Total
Program Managers				
Fundamental changes	16	9	5	30
Independent excursions* . . .	3	3	5	11
Supporting Staff Managers				
Fundamental changes	23	15	3	41
Independent excursions	12	14	4	30
Professionals				
Fundamental changes	15	7	1	23
Independent excursions	2	—	—	2
Total fundamental changes . .	54	31	9	94
Total independent excursions .	17	17	9	43

* For the purpose of this analysis, independent excursions were defined generally as periods of three years or less which bore no apparent relationship, or made no obvious contribution to, the individual's previous or subsequent occupational field.

The professionals were the least mobile with respect to both types of changes. They reported fewer fundamental changes—most of those early in their careers—and almost no independent excursions. But their lack of mobility is hardly surprising. The eight to ten years educational preparation required of a doctor, scientist, lawyer, or economist fairly binds him to the field of his choice.

The supporting staff managers switched occupational fields more often than either the professionals or the program managers. A minority even made fundamental changes late in their careers.

A soil conservationist in Agriculture became a budget officer after fifteen years in the career service and—fourteen years later and in another agency—plied his second career to reach his present post. But the shift from the science of soil conservation to the techniques of budgeting required him to attend two separate courses in budgeting for a total of twenty-six weeks' schooling.

Another supporting staff manager who left his job of twenty-three years as an organic chemist in the development of new drugs to become an industrial liaison officer in the same agency regarded the move as a basic occupational change. In fact, however, his new job involved the working out of "delicate problems with the tobacco, food, and chemical industries," and put to good use his years of experience "at the bench."

Typical experiences of three staff managers illustrate the kinds of independent excursions common to respondents in all three groups.

The Chief of the Compensation Division in the State Department's Office of Personnel spent two of his twenty-five years in federal service (1946, 1947) as a "community action specialist" with the National Housing Agency, and then returned to his original occupational field (personnel).

A staff division director in the Post Office Department's Bureau of Finance worked three years (1955–58) on the staff of the Assistant to the President for Disarmament.

The Chief of the Air Force's Employee Programs Division left personnel work twice during his twenty-five-year career, once in 1937 to become a procurement officer with the Federal Works Agency, and again in 1947 to work as a management analyst with the Veterans Administration. This man, incidentally, has worked in six different bureaus!

Table 14 reveals also that a number of fundamental occupational changes were made by the program managers, some even after twenty years of service. These changes would appear to downgrade the importance of in-depth exposure as a prerequisite for program management, noted in Chapter II. But closer inspection reveals that these changes were not, in most cases, valid occupational switches. They more often illustrated a move from the "bench" level to a post in the same field involving significant supervisory and sometimes program responsibilities. One individual, for example, switched from a position as a practicing labor economist to that of Assistant Director (and then Director) of the United States Employment Service. Another left his job as curator in the Museum of Natural History to become head of the same institution.

Shifts between Principal Groups. In retrospect it is impossible to determine the extent to which individuals have shifted from one group to another, as for example from a supporting-staff manager position to a program manager position. The foregoing illustrations indicate that some have made such shifts. Observation of the sequence of jobs held by the individuals, however, suggests that the proportion who started out in one group and subsequently moved to another group—say, from program manager to staff manager—is relatively small; the proportion who shifted after having attained age thirty is even smaller. In short, our observations suggest that the individual's future role is cast by the time he has completed five years of service.

This suggestion is supported by an analysis of the positions occupied, in July, 1964, by alumni of the Federal Bureau of the Budget who had transferred to another federal agency after having attained grade GS-14 and having served more than five years in the Bureau. Study of the positions in which they served in July, 1964, suggests that once a supporting staff man, always a supporting staff man. A substantial majority of these alumni then served in other federal agencies as staff analyst, budget analyst, accounting officer, and management evalutation officer. In view of the idea cultivated by teachers of public administration in a number of colleges and universities that the Bureau of the Budget is the prime place in which to start a career in the federal service, this observation has special interest. It suggests that many of those who began their careers as "staff" men in the Bureau are often restricted to similar staff positions throughout their careers. And it ignores the fact that experience in the Bureau—in absence of forceful efforts to make the most of talented individuals—*may* provide no more effective development than that available in many other federal agencies.

Experience Outside the Service. Slightly more than one out of ten supergrades have worked outside the federal service since their dates of entry. For most, outside service consisted simply of active duty (one to four years) in military service. For some, it involved exposure to a program or substance-related activity outside the government. The Director of the Civil Aeronautics Board's Safety Bureau, for example, spent 1946 as chief pilot and flight instructor for a small airline. The Assistant Administrator for Real Estate Loans of the Farmers Home Administration worked as a county agriculture agent from 1938 to 1941. And the Deputy Finance Officer for the District of Columbia government worked eleven years outside as a state government employee and as a private consultant.

For some others, however, their outside experience was of questionable value. After attempts at private business, defense relations, or consulting, they returned to government at the same grade or, in a few cases, at cuts in pay.

CAREER GROWTH—THE SUMMING UP

We have pictured the career steps that precede accession to top spots in the federal service. Clearly, there are many routes by which men and women attain the highest positions of trust and responsibility in the career service. But four generalizations can be drawn with respect to these patterns.

1. *The federal government grows its own.* Of the 5,000 now occupying supergrade and PL 313 positions, four-fifths came in below—often at very junior positions—and worked their

way up.[12] Most have spent the better part of their working lives within the career service.[13]

2. *The bulk of tomorrow's managers, supporting staffs, and professionals will continue to come from within.* The small proportion of individuals brought in to the supergrades as lateral entrants (8 per cent of the present group), and the demonstrated reliance on program or functional knowledge suggest that it is unlikely that a significantly larger proportion of those who serve in the upper levels of the civil service as program managers, supporting staffs, or professionals will be recruited into these positions from without the federal service. For the bulk of its top management group, government will look to the lower echelons of the career service to find managers who—on the basis of their knowledge of the program—are able to mold together the forces and groups within and without the agency in the achievement of program objectives. Similarly, it will look below to find staff managers and professionals who possess the experience and understanding of their respective functions or specialties as they apply to the managing of the "public's business."

Yet it is significant that as much as one-fifth of those at the top *did* come in at higher levels (GS-13 and up). These people were brought in to man new and expanding programs, to supply scarce skills, and to prod and stimulate lagging organizations. If experience is any guide, this small but important (and possibly growing) minority will continue to come in to

[12] Eighty per cent came in at grade GS-12 or below. See Appendix B, Appendix Table 17.

[13] Available evidence indicates that, to a large extent, private enterprise also "grows its own." In a survey of 1,700 executives of the nation's largest companies, the editors of *Fortune* found that these executives took some twenty-two years climbing to the top, and that they began in specialized areas (finance, engineering, and law) on the basis of predominantly "practical" educations (85 per cent of the graduates majored in law, business, economics, engineering, or science).

The *Fortune* survey also noted another factor that industrial executives had in common with their federally employed colleagues: long service with their organizations. Only 13 per cent of the *Fortune* respondents were hired from the outside. The bulk of the 1,700 had piled up long years of service—twenty-seven years on the average—with their companies. "1,700 Top Executives," *Fortune*, November, 1959, p. 138.

the government as lateral entrants. For their entry represents, to the government, the most effective and inexpensive means of getting the new blood, especial competence, and large numbers it requires.

3. *The growing up process within the federal service provides but a limited breadth of experience.* The experience of those (76.2 per cent of the total) who have worked throughout their careers in a single occupational field, and those (47.4 per cent of the total) who are still employed in the agency or department by which they were first hired is likely to be especially limited.

The significance of this observation is magnified when it is made clear that, despite the leadership provided by the Civil Service Commission in recent years, only in a small minority of all federal departments, agencies, and bureaus is there any planned effort to promote individuals from job to job from the time they reach grade GS-11 until some achieve supergrade status. "Growing up" within the federal service is characterized by chance and opportunism. Either the individual is at the right place at the right time—employed in an agency when a vacancy appears and apparent to those making the decision—or he seeks out vacancies wherever they may be through friends and professional acquaintances.

This limited experience makes the management job doubly difficult for:

　　—the program manager who must win approval and support from individuals both within and without his program and agency;
　　—the staff manager who represents a government-wide function and who must know, and convince others that he knows, the significance of his function in relation to the program he supports;
　　—the professional who is first a scientist, a lawyer, or an economist, and who must be capable of communicating his knowledge effectively and defending it persuasively both inside and outside the agency.

4. *Since ascent within the federal service is not rapid for most, the problem is how to hold on to the ablest for whose services there is competition.* Rather than put the time "in grade" that is required to advance to the top, some choose to go into industry where the pace, they feel, is more rapid and the rewards for those

who succeed more substantial.[14] Rising family expenditures and the likelihood of greater financial rewards in industry lure them away from the career service. How then, in the light of these obstructions, can government attract the best, and having once gotten them into federal service, can it manage to keep them?

[14] Stanley notes, in discussing the responses of the group he studied to the question: "What do you think are the main reasons that people in your field, at your level, leave the federal service?" that the leading answers were "money," "new worlds to conquer," and "frustrations." Fifty-six per cent cited "more money." Stanley, *op. cit.*, p. 67.

Chapter VI

GETTING AND KEEPING COMPETENCE AT THE TOP

THERE IS A REMARKABLE unanimity of informed opinion that more attention needs be given to maintaining capable men and women in the upper-level career posts in the Executive Branch. The large influence of the relatively few individuals who occupy these positions has been emphasized, during the 1960's, with increasing frequency.[1] And a succession of studies has urged improvement of the processes by which individuals are obtained for these posts and retained in them.[2]

What is to be done about it? This chapter presents some answers to that question. Foregoing chapters have pictured the activities performed by the men and women who make up these staffs. Indirectly, these chapters have revealed the magnitude of the responsibilities borne by many of these individuals. They have, hence, provided a realistic framework within which to consider what needs to be done to maintain capable men and women in upper-level career posts in the Executive Branch. And these chapters have suggested certain guideposts, the recognition of which is essential to any prescriptions for this group.

[1] "Improving Executive Management in the Federal Government," a statement of national policy by the Research and Policy Committee of the Committee for Economic Development, New York, 1964; also Warner *et al.*, *op. cit.*

[2] CED, *op. cit.*, and Stanley, *op. cit.*

GUIDEPOSTS FOR IMPROVEMENT

The determination of what needs to be done requires first the distillation of those generalizations which may serve as guideposts for appraising or designing additional ways to obtain, retain, and strengthen the competences required in top career posts. Six such guideposts are offered here; they relate to the organization of the Executive Branch, the need to balance public and private interests, the art of achieving ends with and through political superiors, the relative requirements for specialized competence of those at the top, the corresponding transferability of "management" or administration among heterogeneous activities, and finally, the role of mobility in federal career planning.

—*Executive Branch Organization.* To many outside the federal service, the misconception prevails that the Executive Branch of the federal government is an integrated, unitary, and closely-knit organization. It is contended that this over-all structure—consisting of more than a dozen departments and over sixty separate agencies, boards, commissions, and the like—is susceptible to single-headed management, much like a large corporate enterprise.

In reality, this degree of order and unity does not exist. The form and location of many federal organizations are products of an admixture of political, technical, and administrative convenience. The relationships among many departments and agencies are numerous and complex. The interfaces among agencies in various fields, such as education, water pollution control, and the elimination of poverty, change and multiply as the federal government's role alters in form, substance, and size.

It follows, hence, that the upper-level civil servant has a large and continuing obligation for "clearance" and coordination. No matter how precisely his responsibility for the accomplishment of a particular set of objectives may be fixed, the program manager, professional, or staff manager is only responsible for a portion of a total governmental effort.

The President of the United States must give leadership to the affairs of the numerous departments, agencies, and boards. For this purpose, he has the aid of his Cabinet (e.g., the Secretary of State), other major political appointees (e.g., Commissioner of Internal Revenue Service, Chairman of the Atomic Energy Commission, Administrator of the Federal Aviation Agency), and a host of organizational, political, and public opinion mechanisms. His task of leadership and coordination is infinitely greater, and quite dissimilar to the task of the corporate executive; the use of such an analogy is simply misleading.

—*Balancing Public and Private Interests.* The upper-level career civil servant must be capable of discharging his responsibilities while charting a course between the Scylla of public interest and the Charybdis of conflicting private interests. Take, for example, the Director of the Bureau of Employment Security in the Department of Labor. Through the administration of grants to the states, he is expected to ensure the existence of a network of public employment offices that will facilitate the finding of jobs for unemployed individuals and the payment of unemployment compensation to workers between jobs. Yet, simultaneously, he is pressed by employers to see that these tasks are conducted in such a manner as to ensure that their individual work forces are not dispersed; he is pressed by organized labor to achieve program objectives in ways that will permit the maintenance of union membership; and he is pressed by organizations of physically disabled workers, of Negroes, and of veterans to ensure that members of each of these groups receive especial aid in finding jobs.

—*Achieving Ends through Political Superiors.* No matter how great the civil servant's professional capabilities, no matter how long his service and how rich his experience, and no matter how clearly recognized his managerial competence, he always occupies a secondary or even tertiary position in the federal service. He must have the added capability of serving effectively, and achieving objectives with and through politically appointed superiors on the basis of a consistent rationale regarding his role in the managerial hierarchy. The essentiality of such a rationale is suggested in a comment by Rufus E. Miles, Jr., Career Assistant Secretary for Administration of the Department of Health, Education, and Welfare:

> A man's first obligation is to represent himself. He should develop a well thought out economic, political, social, and management philosophy and should operate from that foundation. He should listen to those he supervises, but if he disagrees with them, he has the obligation to state his own opinion first to his superiors and then inform them that his staff disagrees and the reasons for their disagreement. Presumably, he is where he is because he has the capacity to lead, not merely take a vote. His view may be worth more than all his subordinates put together. I recall an instance, for example, in which I found that virtually every concerned person in the [department] except I thought that a particular bill ought to be signed. I recommended to the Secretary that it ought to be vetoed. He told me to draft a veto message. The President concurred and sent the veto message to the Congress, and the Congress sustained it. I was not representing any of my subordinates nor any pressure group, but only my concept of the public interest.

—*Requirements for Specialized Competence*. One striking fact, apparent in the careers of those program managers, supporting staff managers, and professionals examined in this study, is that almost to a man their present competence rests largely on the earlier foundations of particularized experience in a program or substantive field. Nearly all in the sample have been long exposed to their chosen programs and disciplines. Most demonstrated their particular *managerial* competence in terms of their ability to deal with, and give order to, a wide range of specialized or program-related problems. Seldom were the answers to management problems or the directions for management action the product of only a generalist-type exposure to, and attack on, the problems at hand.[3]

In a real sense, these men and women were involved in the warp and woof of the substantive fabric of their programs and disciplines. It has become increasingly apparent that the complex questions of policy, program, personnel, and cost that

---

[3] The fact that there is need for both program knowledge and administrative technique was noted by both Lewis Meriam and O. Glenn Stahl in the 1930's. See, for example, "Public Service Training in Universities," by Stahl, *American Political Science Review*, October, 1937.

individuals at or near the top must decide cannot be dealt with in the vacuums of a broad liberal viewpoint or a capacity for administration. They must be decided in terms of the technical realities of the program.

—*Transferability of Management Skills.* Yet, in this group of top-level civil servants, there are those who have moved across organizational and occupational bounds, sometimes at late and fairly senior points in their careers. For example, the Director of the Federal Home Loan Bank Operations Division of the Home Loan Bank Board, who has served in three bureaus throughout his twenty-five year career, was working in the Internal Revenue Service in 1952 and in the Navy Department as late as 1954. The Chief of the Federal Power Commission's Office of Economics, a veteran of twenty-five years of federal service, served in the Treasury Department as late as 1962. And a late switch in occupations: the Deputy Director for Foreign Buildings Operations in the Department of State assumed his present job in 1963, after having spent fifteen years in budget and finance, and twelve years before that in soil conservation!

These examples represent a minority of those at the top of the federal service.[4] They illustrate the exception rather than the rule. Generally, in any organization, public or private, the *bulk* of those at the top will have arrived by dint of conscious mastery of the substance of their programs or disciplines *and* by the application, in their chosen fields, of acquired management skills. The few—the very few—who violate the rule represent unique and extraordinary competence *or* fortuitous circumstance.

The experiences of these exceptional few should not be generalized for all those in even this exclusive group of civil servants. The skills of planning, budgeting, controlling, and the like are applied most effectively, in the main, by those who understand the milieu in which they operate. Viewed in this

---

[4] Approximately 5 per cent of all those in this study changed bureaus *after* ten years in federal service.

light, requisite management abilities are clearly supplemental to the essential mastery of the program or the discipline.[5]

—*Mobility in Career Planning.* As this study has shown,[6] the recorded experience of those at the top of the federal service today has been deeper than it has been broad. Relatively few of those at the top have served in more than one or two bureaus, or have acquired backgrounds in more than a single occupational field or program.

Yet, two factors argue strongly that those in responsible positions can benefit from broader exposure to related programs and problems. The first is the aforementioned growth in the complexity and interrelatedness of many federal programs (e.g., resources management, education, poverty) and the consequent demand for managers and staff who have the capacity to see beyond the parochialism of their own bureau or program.

The second factor is related to the first. It is the need for a broader utilization and development of the raw materials from which top managers are made. The federal government is fortunate in having—for any function or program—a number of organizations in which the competent and promising individual with a bent for a particular program field or specialty can fit. The expansion of career opportunities across organizational but still within functional or program lines provides increased incentive to the "mover," to the up-and-coming specialist or middle manager who seeks constantly increasing

[5] In *The Performing Arts: Problems and Prospects*, the Rockefeller Panel Report on the future of theatre, dance, music in America (New York: McGraw-Hill Book Co., 1965), the question is asked, "What constitutes a good manager in this field [i.e., the arts]?" The question is answered in these words, "He has been described by an authority on the subject as a man 'who must be knowledgeable in the art with which he is concerned, an impresario, labor negotiator, diplomat, educator, publicity and public relations expert, politician, skilled businessman, a social sophisticate, a servant of the community, a tireless leader—becomingly humble before authority —a teacher, a tyrant, and a continuing student of the arts.' " (p. 161) Copyright © 1965 by Rockefeller Brothers Fund, Inc. Reprinted by permission of McGraw-Hill Book Company.

[6] See Chapter V, pp. 116–117.

opportunity and responsibility.[7] The provision of increased mobility within these bounds can do much to retain, in federal service, many who would otherwise be lost to positions outside the government.

These six guideposts provide a necessary framework within which the especial nature of the competences required by those who are to serve in the upper levels of the federal service can be viewed. They provide, moreover, an introduction to the improvements we recommend in the ways of recruiting, compensating, and developing those on their way to the top.

DEFINING THE COMPETENCES REQUIRED

Two observations by an authority on management, Henri Fayol,[8] nearly fifty years ago, point the way toward needed improvements. His first observation is that effective performance in any position above the beginning level in an organizational hierarchy requires of the individual a combination of skills and understandings. The second observation is that, as one rises in the hierarchy, the mix of skills and understandings required varies markedly.

Chapters II, III, and IV illustrate that the activities and nature of the responsibilities of the *program manager* differ from

[7] Available evidence indicates that similar factors influence the motivations and actions of aggressive, capable, and rising young managers in private industry. The first of a series of articles in *Fortune* entitled, "The Young Executive," characterizes the young executive as: "aggressive, confident, independent, and decisive—all qualities that seem to have been part of his natural character and mental structure since he began to mature. He possesses an inquiring, acquisitive mind that he has trained and polished until it has become an extraordinarily effective instrument with which to attack the entwined problems of his business life. He works hard, partly because competitive fires burn within him, partly because he forever seeks 'more challenge and more responsibility,' and he believes hard work can attain for him those twin desiderata. He has a strong propensity toward pragmatism— he strives always to effect changes in the external world, changes that he can then hold out at arm's length and admire." *Fortune*, June, 1964, p. 98.

[8] Henri Fayol, *General and Industrial Management*, (London: Sir Isaac Pitman & Sons, Ltd., 1949), Chapter II, pp. 7–13.

those of the *supporting staff manager* and from those of the *professional*. To perform effectively in one type of position requires a different combination of skills and understandings than are required in another type of position. The combination of skills and understanding differs because of the different responsibilities borne by those who serve in top program, support, and professional posts. As summarized in Chapter V, the responsibilities of each group vary in terms of ultimacy, source of authority and focus, nature and breadth of span of control, and finally—the extent to which authority is subject to challenge.

Similarly, the combination of skills and understandings required of the individual varies from one program field to another (from public health administration, say, to the enforcement of antitrust laws), and from one function to another (from personnel to procurement).

Consider, for example, the respective careers of two program managers: John Wason, Director of Travel Promotion for the United States Travel Service, and Joe Browning, Technical Director of the Naval Propellant Plan. Mr. Wason was a political science graduate who now sells foreigners on travel in the United States and maintains contacts with state and local officials, advertising executives, and others who will aid him in achieving this objective, because to them tourism is vital. Mr. Browning was a chemistry graduate who now directs a 2,800-man staff of scientists, technicians, and support people; his milieu includes esoteric technical terms and multimillion dollar research outlays.

Henri Fayol's second observation, about the different skills needed as men rise in the hierarchy, is also illustrated by the case histories in earlier chapters. One must take into account differing activities of individuals who serve at the three supergrade levels and the career steps by which these individuals reached the top.

Most who reach top career posts entered at low levels as accountants, attorneys, economists, engineers, physicists, budgeteers, and the like. Their advance was gradual: Few at the beginning had the skills and understanding required of the man who can assume responsibility for planning the development of a supersonic transport or for steering legislation to provide medical care for the aged; or for supervising a 60,000-man staff (as does the Deputy Commissioner of IRS), winning the support of constituencies (as did a respondent from the Veterans Administration), or having to represent their specialized function before the departmental secretary or the Congress (as did many supporting staff managers and some professionals). Most were acquainted only with a specialized segment of the activity of their agency. Those who came in part-way up the career ladder, after previous service in private enterprise or a university, brought different combinations of skills and understanding, but seldom that particular combination required in the position they entered.

What must be done to maintain capable managerial and professional staffs in the Executive Branch is suggested by the adaptation of a table presented originally by Fayol in 1916. It shows, broadly, the skills and understandings required of the career civil servant as he ascends the hierarchal ladder. To be sure, this communicates only a very general idea; neither the vertical nor horizontal dimensions of the chart convey a precise measure of the individual's ascent or the skills and understanding he requires. Nor do we claim to have identified the differences inherent in the positions of program manager, supporting staff manager, and professional. That there *are* differences is our contention.

The *vertical dimension* of the chart depicts the working life span of the career program manager, supporting staff manager, or professional. It suggests that the beginner in the federal career service—as an aide to a program manager, as a staff assistant, or as a junior scientist—will spend his time on narrow, apprentice-like assignments during his first years of employment. Only a very few are fortunate enough to be assigned to posts that afford them a panoramic view of the agency's operations.

After three to seven years, the apprentice graduates to the first professional level (grade GS-13 or thereabouts). There he assumes responsibilities for planning and supervising the

UNDERSTANDINGS REQUIRED BY THE PUBLIC SERVANT *
On His Way Up in the Career Service

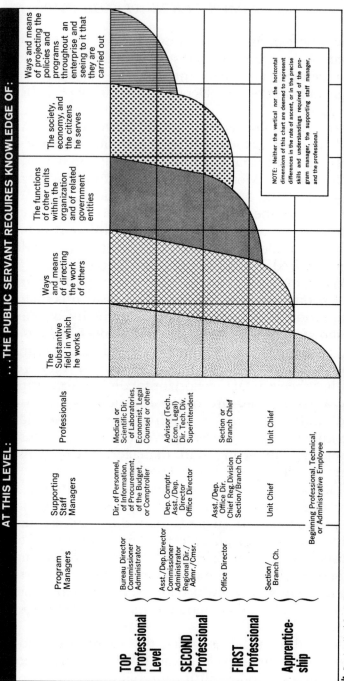

NOTE: Neither the vertical nor the horizontal dimensions of this chart are deemed to represent differences in the rate of ascent, or in the precise skills and understandings required of the program manager, the supporting staff manager, and the professional.

* Based on Henri Fayol's Table II. "Relative Importance of Requisite Abilities of Personnel in Industrial Concerns," in *General and Industrial Management* (London: Sir Isaac Pitman & Sons, Ltd., 1949), p. 10. Adapted, with permission of the American Society for Public Administration, from the Chart appearing in "Equipping Men for Career Growth in the Public Service," by John J. Corson, *Public Administration Review*, March, 1963, p. 2.

work of others, of representing his unit in negotiations with spokesmen for other organizational units, and of speaking for his staff to those who will prescribe its work, determine its budget, and evaluate its performance. These added tasks require of the individual new skills and greater understanding.[9] The general nature of these new skills and understandings is suggested by the *horizontal dimension* of this chart.

The average federal career servant attains the second professional level (made up principally of those in grades GS-14 and GS-15) after eight to twelve years in the public service. Here, he typically serves as chief of a large branch, assistant chief of a large division (or a chief of a smaller one), or as principal advisor to a deputy administrator of an agency. At this level, he is responsible for directing the work of more people and, importantly, of individuals from diverse disciplines. His responsibility for representing the unit he heads requires that he understand the functions of other units in the agency, board, or department in which he serves and the programs of other government entities operating in the same field. His attention must turn outward. Though he must still devote the bulk of his time to his staff, he increasingly pays attention to his relationships with other divisions of his own agency or department, with other departments, and with constituent groups and to the problems they present.[10]

Finally, after fifteen to twenty years in the federal service, the career man—if successful—moves to the top. He reaches a

[9] Obviously, there are those in all three categories who come in better educated or more experienced than their peers. For some, this "first professional level" may constitute the entry level. For others, the apprenticeship period may be foreshortened from years to months if their qualifications and output warrant it.

[10] *The New York Times* described on Sunday, February 21, 1965, the career of Donald N. Frey, general manager of the Ford Division of the Ford Motor Company. Mr. Frey entered the employ of the Ford Motor Company as manager of the metallurgy department of the company's scientific laboratory. Successive assignments over the next fourteen years acquainted Mr. Frey with the research management, engineering, product planning, marketing, and financial aspects of the production and distribution of the automobiles that make up the Ford line, and that line alone. The combination of skills and understandings suggested by Mr. Frey's career and his present position offer an analogy to that of the top-level federal career servant.

position such as Executive Director of the Federal Power Commission, Deputy Treasurer of the United States, Director of the Civil Aeronautics Board's Bureau of Economic Regulation, or Economic Advisor to the Secretary of Agriculture. At this topmost level of the career service, he requires a vast comprehension of the program or function in which he is looked to as a leader, an understanding of those programs and substantive fields that bear directly on his own, *and* a deep understanding of the processes by which he must motivate and mobilize human beings to the fulfillment of the broad purposes to which his program or function is addressed. The successful man, at this level, possesses a unique combination of skills and understandings[11] that equip him to handle effectively technical problems welling up from a staff comprised of many disciplines (e.g., in the field of social security, or in the field of international affairs).[12] He must be able to plan, direct, and control the activities of a large staff, and to deal effectively with powerful interest groups and legislative bodies and to gain and hold their respect.

RECRUITING FOR UPPER-LEVEL POSITIONS

In decade 1965–75, at least 4,000 individuals with the skills and understandings that have been suggested will be required:

—to replace those men and women now occupying top-level positions who will retire, die, resign, or be dismissed, and

[11] Frederick R. Kappel, Chairman of the Board, American Telephone and Telegraph Company, in a speech given at the Centennial Dinner of the Columbia University's School of Engineering entitled, "What Do We Need Most from Engineers?" speaks of the need of the engineer "to comprehend the market" and "to have an intelligent, broad-visioned political attitude."

[12] As previously noted, the skills required of the program manager, the supporting staff manager, and the professional stem from the number of disciplines represented in the staff the individual directs. The program manager must interrelate the efforts of individuals from several disciplines; the supporting staff manager and the professional direct the efforts of individuals, most of whom are trained in a single discipline.

—to fill new positions (many requiring professional skills not now found in the federal service) that will be established as the federal government assumes new functions and grows in size.

During the decade ended on January 31, 1965, the total number of individuals serving at these topmost levels of the federal career civil service grew from approximately 1,175 to about 4,890. Almost three of every four of the individuals now serving in these positions entered the federal service at be-ginning-level jobs, with little work experience prior to entry. Most were recruited upon the completion of their educations and entered the federal service to serve as junior accountants, biologists, engineers, lawyers, and physicists, or in other special-ized posts.

The conditions under which young people are brought into the career service today are manifestly different from those that prevailed in the past. The buyers' market of the 1930's ceased to exist a good many years ago. The federal govern-ment is now—and has been for sometime—in a sellers' market. (Many contend that there will always be a sellers' market for top talent.)

Yet, to an alarming extent, the government has relied on the reservoir of talent selected in the thirties and has never out-grown the attitude that it could simply wait for people to apply and then select the best of those who present themselves. Selection is possible in a buyers' market; recruitment—effec-tively thought out and aggressively pursued—is essential in a sellers' market. But the personnel system of the federal govern-ment is implicitly constructed on the basis of selecting from among those who present themselves rather than competing with A.T.&T. and General Motors for a scarce commodity.

What must be done to improve federal recruiting efforts? What steps must be taken to ensure that annual input[13] to the

---

[13] During the early 1960's, the number of college graduate entrants to the federal civil service (those with the bachelor's and higher degrees) has ranged from 15,000 to 22,500 a year. This total comprises a large variety of occupational categories; among the occupations represented were: accountants (perhaps 10 per cent of total), biologists (9 per cent), business administrators (15 per cent), lawyers (9 per cent), engineers and physical scientists (26 per cent), social scientists including psychologists and social workers (8–12 per cent), and others. The foregoing per-

career service includes a requisite number of individuals with the talents required for service at the topmost levels of the career service two decades hence?

First, there is need for institutionalized foresight—for forecasting the number that will likely be required for each kind and occupational category of position that can be foreseen.[14] The forecasting will not be good,[15] but periodic revision of such forecasts will do much to aid those involved with staffing to think out what steps should be taken to provide and train the human resources that will be required five and even ten years in the future.

Second, there is need for imaginative research to aid recruiters in identifying, at the entry levels, those talents and value orientations that will contribute to the development of this raw material as the years pass and will ensure the proper mix of new people to handle the variety of responsibilities to be borne in the future (program leadership, supporting staff service, professional counsel, research and inquiry and so forth). There is evidence that those who excel in academic work may not include equal proportions of individuals:

> (a) willing and desirous of working within, and achieving leadership of, groups of individuals;
> (b) content to gain, hold, and increase acceptance by other members of their work group, as a necessary prerequisite to achieving program and organizational goals;

---

centages are rough estimates designed to reveal the approximate representation of occupational categories. Each of the categories is further subdivided in the recruitment process; "lawyers," for example, includes tax examiners, legal instruments examiners, claims examiners, trade mark examiners, and investigators. See "Federal Service Entrance Examination, General Register Appointment Activity," for periods January 1, 1962, through December 31, 1962, and January 1, 1963, through December 31, 1963.

[14] A start has been made; see the United States Civil Service Commission's *Federal Workforce Outlook, Fiscal Years 1965–1968*, November, 1964. The next step needed is forecasting by each department and agency.

[15] In 1964, one of the authors participated in planning and assembling such forecasts by the heads of each department of the California state government. The results reflected a tendency to underestimate prospective growth and little ability to foresee the new professional skills likely to be required. But the effort to forecast the professional personnel required significantly contributed to the sharpening of program plans.

(c) dedicated to a system of social, religious, or political ideals, and likely to provide the zeal, if not intellectual leadership, that may be required for program advance;

(d) insistent upon the right to structure their own activities and to be as free as possible from the pressure, direction, or interference of others.[16]

This need for continuing research is not new or unrecognized. The need is to find ways of refining the recruitment of young specialists to ensure the availability two decades later of a requisite number of broad-gauged, top-level civil servants capable of serving in a variety of responsible posts.

Third, the federal government needs to alter drastically its concept and methods of recruiting if it is to obtain an adequate number of persons who have the capacities to become distinguished career leaders in the decades ahead. The need is to outgrow the idea that one can sit around and wait for talent to beat down the doors. The race for quality is a rigorous one to be run by only the best runners. The federal government needs to send out its most knowledgeable and persuasive career people to do the recruiting—the managers who run exciting and challenging programs and the professionals whose vision (and persuasiveness) includes a deepfelt enthusiasm for the substance of the work they do. This vital task of finding and attracting those who are good and who have the capacity to grow is too important to be left to the professional recruiters and the personnel offices.

Finally, there is the need for recruiting individuals with special skills from private life immediately into supergrade positions. The need is for a larger number than have been recruited in recent years. For as the numbers and varieties of specializations and programs increase, an adequate supply of specialists may not be generated within the government. This need was recognized by the enactment of Public Law 313; sponsors of that statute argued that the Department of Defense required the authority to pay higher salaries than were pre-

[16] E. Ginzberg and J. L. Herma, in *Talent and Performance* (New York: Columbia University Press, 1964), show that such "value orientations" markedly influenced the career choices and accomplishments of a group of superior graduate students of the Columbia University during the ten to fifteen years after they had left the University.

vailing in 1947 (when this legislation was enacted) to enable them to attract needed scientists and engineers directly from civilian life into career civil service posts.

Of those now serving in the three highest grades of the career service 7 per cent entered at supergrade levels. Of this 7 per cent, the predominant proportion includes men and women of a high order of innate ability, extensive education, and a relatively unique work experience. A large proportion of this number were educated and experienced as doctors, lawyers, scientists, economists, and statisticians.[17]

Such lateral-entry recruitment needs to be encouraged in the future. As the federal government grows and undertakes new functions (such as underwater exploration), there will be increasing requirements for individuals with skills not heretofore used in government.[18] To meet this need and to provide the stimulus for those already in the public service that is afforded by the competition of the new faces with the old hands long in the federal service, there is need for recruiting a significantly larger proportion in the future directly from private employment into supergrade posts.

Lateral entry may well vary in the extent to which it can be accomplished and in the areas in which it is most appropriate. To bring in scarce scientific skills, for example, has been found to be a legitimate application of the concept. On the other hand, there would be little utility in bringing in from the outside a tax specialist or an accountant when—and we believe this to be true—these skills can be better developed from within.

COMPENSATION OF MEN AT THE TOP

The effectiveness of recruitment at the entry level will always depend in some degree on the relative level of compensation

[17] Of the thirty respondents in this study who comprise the 7 per cent of the total sample studied, eleven held the Ph.D. degree, five held law degrees, and four, Master's degrees.

[18] The National Aeronautics and Space Administration offers a striking example of a new program, the staffing of which required going outside for top talent. More than one-third of the men for its top twenty-two management spots were recruited into their positions from outside the government.

that prevails, not only for beginners, but for those at the topmost level of the federal service. The beginners—particularly the best of them—often will look not only at the beginning salary, but at the compensation they can hope to obtain if they succeed over a lifetime.

The compensation of those who serve at the topmost levels of the federal civil service has long been notoriously low. It has been low in relation to the earnings of those performing analogous work for private profit-making employers, and even in relation to the earnings of those performing analogous tasks for some nonprofit agencies, educational institutions, and some municipal governments.[19] It has been low in relation to the earnings of those in the secretarial, clerical, and beginning professional ranks of the federal civil service.[20] For example, the private executive earning $75,000 to $100,000 per annum will probably receive ten to twelve times the annual earnings of his secretary; the federal top-level career servant earning $21,000 to $28,000 receives only three or four times the earnings of his secretary.

The level of compensation of those who serve in these positions has been held low by the insistence of members of Congress that the highest salary for a career civil servant shall not exceed that of a Congressman. It has been held low, too, by the erroneous notion held generally by Americans that it is not necessary to provide compensation roughly equivalent to the average (not the very highest) compensation paid to individuals performing analogous work in private enterprise.

During recent years significant progress has been made in raising the pay of top-level civil servants, as shown by these figures on salary levels:

[19] This fact was demonstrated by the Randall Commission. And it was demonstrated for another group of upper-level public servants—the occupants of top-level positions in the New York State Civil Service—by an unpublished study made by McKinsey & Company, Inc., in 1962, for Governor Nelson Rockefeller, and used by the Governor as a basis for recommendations for increased salary levels.

[20] See, for example, analyses presented by John J. Corson in "Comparable Pay for Comparable Work?," *Public Administration Review*, Vol. 21, No. 4, Autumn, 1961, pp. 198–205.

	in 1955	and	*in 1965*
Grade GS-18	$14,800		$24,500
Grade GS-17	$13,975–$14,620		$21,445–$24,445
Grade GS-16	$12,900–$13,760		$18,935–$24,175

If, in the future, the federal government is to provide compensation sufficient to attract and hold individuals competent to discharge the responsibilities that devolve on men and women serving in the three highest echelons of the career service, two compensation policies must be implemented.

First, a means needs to be perfected for comparing, each year, the level of federal compensation with that prevailing for individuals performing analogous tasks in nongovernmental employment. Prevailing policy holds that federal civil servants serving in posts classified up to grade GS-16 shall receive compensation roughly equivalent to their counterparts in private enterprise. This policy was written into legislation in the Salary Reform Act of 1962. To "perfect" the implementation of this policy will require gradual improvement of means of comparing the compensation of upper-level jobs in government with compensation in analogous upper-level positions.

Technicians have long held that it is difficult or impossible effectively to compare the responsibilities of the topmost positions in government with positions in private enterprise. Yet, ways must be found and a rationale developed to provide a guide that will permit the approximation of "comparable pay for comparable work" even for positions at grades GS-16, -17, and -18 of the federal career service.

Second, there is need for the modification of existing promotional policies and practices to expedite the advance of those individuals who demonstrate special capabilities and promise.

Of those individuals now serving at the topmost levels in the federal career service who started in positions classified at grades GS-9 or lower, a minority had attained grade GS-16 when they completed twenty years of service. This presents a critical problem, for two basic reasons. The individual possessing talent and ambition is often impatient at such slow advancement; he will seek employment where advance is more rapid. Furthermore, this period, from approximately twenty-five to forty-five years of age, is the one during which family responsibilities and income needs—particularly during the last five years—are growing. If compensation does not keep pace, pressure upon the individual to seek employment elsewhere is increased; worse, the venturesomeness and creative urges of the individual are lessened by economic stress.

This chapter has presented six guideposts that will help in appraising what has been done and in planning what need be done to obtain and retain capable men and women in the upper-level career posts in the Executive Branch of the federal government. It has suggested also the next steps that need to be taken in the improvement of recruitment and compensation processes. But these two steps, while consequential, will not determine the calibre of the individuals who, through experience and demonstrated growth, rise to upper-level career positions. Hence, in the next and concluding chapter, we turn to the principal means by which the calibre of upper-level civil servants is determined.

Chapter VII

DEVELOPING THE
TALENT REQUIRED

THE MAJORITY of the men who will occupy important top-level civil service posts in 1975 are now in the federal service. Whether they will be equipped for the posts they then occupy is being determined *now* by the processes by which:

    —each is assigned and reassigned work to be done;
    —some are selected for promotion and others passed over;
    —all are trained and developed for their ultimate responsibilities.

Men do not become program managers, supporting staff specialists, or professional administrators or advisors overnight. They must be groomed—and they must groom themselves—for top positions that may be achieved a score of years later. That grooming is a career-long process. It commences, or should commence, when the individual identifies himself (or often by chance is identified) with a particular program, such as the administration of the national parks; with a supporting staff specialty, such as budgetary administration, or with a professional field, for example, the law. The grooming proceeds throughout the years, by chance or by design.

The fortunate individual identifies himself with an organizational unit or with a supervisor who accepts, as part of the supervisor's task, responsibility for developing each employee's capabilities to the fullest. The less fortunate but equally talented individual takes upon himself the job of developing his own capabilities. But what is the substance of this development? What body of understanding must the individual acquire to advance?

To equip himself for a top-level career position a score of years hence, the individual who advances in the federal service must continually acquire an ever broader and deeper programmatic "base." Simultaneously, he must develop an "overlay" that includes familiarity with the internal and external environment in which he operates and a solid grasp of administrative and executive skills and processes. This is the lesson that Fayol taught a half century ago, and communicated through the chart we have presented. And the lesson taught is affirmed by the analyses presented in Chapters II, III, and IV of the varied activities of those now serving in top-career positions.

FOUR ADDED ELEMENTS

The building of this base and overlay begins, for most individuals, before their entry into federal service. In graduate and undergraduate study, most who subsequently enter the federal service obtain at least textbook knowledge of an area of specialization. A few gain, in addition, an acquaintance with the environment within which federal employees work, and with the processes of administration. But, there are four elements to be added, the learning of which requires that the individual be involved in the "doing" of the jobs.

The Capacity for Directing Others

The apprentice who brings to the service a beginner's knowledge of some specialization, perhaps accounting or cryptology, must shortly acquire an understanding of *work direction.* The apprentice must learn to supervise the activities of others for whose work he is responsible. The term "supervision" accurately connotes the face-to-face relationship that obtains at the highest and the lowest levels of the organization. He learns that this process involves:

(a) an understanding of the expectations, values, and interpersonal skills of his subordinates, and

(b) an ability to communicate (and to be communicated with) in three directions—downward to one's subordinates, laterally to equals, and upward to superiors to whom he represents his subordinates.

As the employee moves up the career ladder, the tasks of work direction become more complex.[1] The now promoted apprentice must direct the efforts of others who are *not* in the room, but perhaps halfway across the United States, and who represent several skills in which he, as director, is not expert. Increasingly, he must achieve the ends of his organization through people who are not his subordinates, but from whom he must win support, get advice or approval. His skills as a representative, bargainer, or negotiator need be developed.

Understanding the Internal Environment

"The memoirs of almost any president of a major corporation," Wight Bakke wrote a decade ago, "will include a description of experiences in getting the sales, production, and comptroller's departments together in the solution of a particular company problem."[2] The corporation president's experience is duplicated by that of many top-level career civil servants. The activities of several of those studied reflect the problem posed by division and bureau heads who identify themselves with the programs, manpower needs, or budgets of their respective divisions or bureaus. A federal supergrade incumbent spends much time countering the Ptolemaic outlooks of his staff members, helping them to see that the bureau or department does not revolve around their respective divisions or bureaus.

---

[1] For analyses of the nature of these tasks, see Rensis Likert, *New Patterns of Management* (New York: McGraw-Hill Book Company, Inc., 1961), Chapters 7 and 12.

[2] E. Wight Bakke, *Bonds of Organization* (New York: Harper & Bros., 1951), p. 19.

The man who becomes a first line supervisor learns quickly the underside of this problem. If his wits are about him, he learns that he must know what each other unit of the enter-prise—the personnel office, the budget office, the comptroller's office, the training division, the treasurer and the auditors, and particularly the other substantive (or operating) units—is doing. It is not enough that he knows *what* these units do: it is essential that he knows *why* they think the way they do. The need for such understanding is reflected in the curricula of most university executive development programs. Unfor-tunately, analysis of these curricula will reveal that some programs offer *only* illumination of this single segment of the lore the individual requires.

Understanding the External Environment

The career employee who rises to the top of the federal service must develop an understanding of the external en-vironment in which his agency operates. This may involve, for the Economic Adjustment Advisor in Defense, an appreciation of the effects of base closings on local communities and indus-tries. For the Vietnam desk officer in State, it requires a knowledge of the vague and conflicting views of the Bhuddist, Catholic, and military groups in that country. For the district director of the Internal Revenue Service, it may entail a con-certed and continual effort to build acceptance and support for the Service among businessmen and private citizens in the community.

The most obvious reason why the individual, as he rises in the federal service, requires an understanding of this external realm is that his decisions affect the lives of many citizens who make up this environment. The second reason is that most federal employees spend their entire careers in a single program or function; thousands live in Washington, mingle only with other federal employees, and are isolated in principal part from the constituents they serve and who are affected by their actions.

The third reason is that the civil servant, hemmed in most of a working lifetime by exposure only to that part of the external realm that he and his agency serve, acquires a myopic view of the society of which his constituency is only a part. The specialist in highway planning for the Bureau of Public Roads has but a limited appreciation for the problems of those urban dwellers displaced from the slums through which his highways cut. It takes an eminently broad-gauged man in the position of Chief Forester of the United States not to become unduly impressed with the special and often conflicting concerns of the lumber manufacturers, the graziers, the recreationists, and others who have pressed their views on him over a lifetime of public service.

A few beginners bring to their assignments in government a textbook understanding of governmental structure, of the role of the legislature, of the relationship of government to the individual, of the structure of the American society that government serves, and of the impact of government on the economy and on the individual enterprise. This textbook understanding is expanded, tested, and distorted by their experiences (most of them secondary) during the years they work their way up through the apprenticeship, the first and the second professional levels of the service. Consequently, their need for understanding of the external environment becomes acute, whether they realize it or not, by the time they reach the second professional level.

For many, this need is manifested by a deepfelt belief that the Legislative Branch, the congressional committee, and the individual Congressman are the natural enemies, or at least opponents, of the Executive Branch, the department or bureau, and the career executive. It is manifested, too, by a minimum of understanding of the Congressman as a voice for his constituents, as a legislative committee member, or as a candidate for election and re-election.

Understanding Management

The activities of those who serve at the topmost levels of the federal service reveal the amalgam that management is in the daily life of a federal career man. Analysis of these activities shows that the upper-level career servant is deeply involved in the substance of the program with which he is associated. It shows that the decisions he makes as to plans, personnel, budget, physical facilities, or procurement (presumably the warp and woof of management) are inextricably intertwined with a comprehensive understanding of the program itself.

The individual who is not intellectually conversant with the specializations over which he presides serves only as a rubber stamp approving decisions made by his subordinates. He seldom holds the respect of associates who recognize that he doesn't really know what they are talking about. To win and hold their respect, the manager must demonstrate a belief in and even dedication to the agency's program, and a working knowledge of the specialities his staff possesses.[3] Jacques Barzun has stated the feasibility of such an understanding in these eloquent words:

> The universal formula is "You cannot understand or appreciate my art (science) (trade) unless you yourself practice it." This error is briskly propagated by the schools, in the name of scholarship and with genuflections before the menacing heap of knowledge, of which no man can appropriate more than a little. We forget that every age has carried with it great loads of information, most of it false or tautological, yet deemed indispensable at the time. Of true knowledge at any time, a good part is merely convenient, necessary indeed to the worker, but not to an understanding of his subject: one can judge a building without knowing where to buy the bricks; one can understand a violin sonata without knowing how to score for the instrument. The work may in fact be better understood *without* a knowledge of the details of its manufacture, for attention to these tends to distract from meaning and effect. Even if one sets apart those arts and sciences that require special preparation, there remains a large field to which Intellect has access in its own right. With a cautious confidence and sufficient intellectual training, it is possible to master the literature of a subject and gain a proper understanding of it: . . . This will not enable one to add to what is known, but it will give possession of *all that the discipline has to offer the world.*[4]

[3] John F. Kennedy, in April, 1958, when serving as a Senator from Massachusetts, told an audience honoring the Rockefeller Public Service Award winners of that year that without civil servants concerned about current issues, the Congress effectively is in the position of "the bland leading the bland."

[4] Jacques Barzun, *The House of Intellect* (New York: Harper & Bros., 1959), pp. 11–12.

A private business executive may manage men and money and leave the substance of the business to his colleagues, although few successful private business executives do. But a public administrator cannot. He must grapple with the substance of the specialties and the content of the program that utilizes them all.

He must learn how to project his plans to thousands of employees he may never see face to face, in simple, intelligible language that will gain cooperation and stimulate zeal, and then he must continually learn what they are doing and how well. He must learn how to interpret and to sell the activity for which he is responsible to numerous constituencies within the body politic, without becoming the tool of any constituency. He must acquire a progressively heightened understanding of what is in the minds of his employees, other governmental executives, congressional committee members, and constituency spokesmen with whom he must deal.

The analysis of the activities of the upper-level civil servant shows that he is continually striving to mould a team out of subordinates, peers, and others in and out of the agency, and simultaneously is performing an entrepreneurial function,[5] that of formulating out of prior experience proposals for new legislation, policies, processes and procedures, and then of advancing these by negotiating within and without. This latter half of the entrepreneurial function emphasizes the critical importance of communications skills. The upper-level civil servant must not only convey ideas to scientists, economists, lawyers, competing managers, politicians, industry representatives, and private citizens, but he also must persuade them if he is to advance his program.

REQUIRING SUSTAINED GROWTH

The individual who would succeed to the top of the federal career service faces the reality that his own development is a

---

[5] Drucker, *op. cit.*, has made a notable contribution to thinking about management in differentiating between the executive function of management (i.e., the carrying out of existing policies and programs) and the entrepreneurial function of management (i.e., the initiation, formulation, gaining acceptance, and implementation of new policies, programs, and processes).

career-long process. And if the career service is to sustain the quality of this top group, the merits of tenure must be weighed against the requirement that the individual continue to grow (and show by his performance that he has grown) throughout his entire career.

Career-Long Development

How does the individual who pursues a career in the federal civil service acquire the amalgam of understandings he requires? And how can the process of development be improved?

a) *Developing by Doing*

Much that the individual rising within the federal service needs to know, he can and should learn by being involved. The city planner, for example, probably an engineer or architect by training, needs to study urban economics and sociology. But he will never know his city until he has been involved in its economic and social life and has come to know firsthand the factors that influence businessmen in locating branch stores, office buildings, and factories; the factors that are important to welfare and police officials in deploying their forces and facilities; and the problems that plague traffic engineers. He can learn much by reading, but there is much he must learn through his forearms, with his sleeves rolled above his elbows.

How much the individual will learn through being involved depends upon the character of successive assignments and the rapidity with which he is given more challenging assignments. Today, the federal career servant's development is too much dependent on chance—the chance that he finds an opening in an agency which is expanding and growing. In such agencies, the likelihood that the individual will grow as a result of being pushed into a succession of challenging assignments is large, e.g., NASA within the period 1958 through 1962. But the growth of many individuals is limited by the lack of opportunities for advancement, e.g., the Federal Power Commission from 1956–60.

The federal career employee's development also depends on the chance that successive assignments and jobs provide constructive supervision and leadership and confront him with new and exacting problems that progressively build on what he has learned in previous assignments. If the individual has the good fortune to work with a succession of bosses who delegate fully, set exacting standards, and hold him fully accountable, he will probably develop to the fullest of his capabilities. If he has the ill luck to be assigned to a succession of bosses who delegate little, whose own standards of performance are low, and who accept little or no responsibility for the growth of those whom they supervise, he will probably not develop his capabilities to the fullest. And invaluable talent is tragically lost in the federal government because of middle-management supervisors' failure to stimulate and train those whose careers are entrusted to them.

b) *Developing by Moving*

But mobility for mobility's sake contributes little to the individual's development. Indeed it can breed a superficiality that limits subsequent effectiveness and denies the individual the opportunity to accumulate those related skills and understandings which progressive assignments within a related field or fields can contribute.

If a *program manager* is to acquire the requisite understanding of the program itself and of the internal and external environments through which he will get things done, and if at the same time he is to acquire the capacity for directing the work of the specialists found in his particular field, he can only reach this level after a succession of assignments which contribute these several understandings. If a *supporting staff manager* is to possess the requisite understanding of the specialized service he provides (be it personnel administration, finance, or procurement), he should reach the top through a succession of assignments that develop his understanding of, and skill in, the specialization *and* his familiarity with the program fields in which he would apply it.

The notion that mobility *per se* is good persists. This notion stems from the legacy of the administrative class within the British civil service. Yet, a member of the British administrative class has eloquently pointed out that in his country the evolution of governmental functions has substantially made obsolete this notion of general mobility, of the interchangeable administrator.

> Interchangeability presupposes [he has written] a set of ideal men in an amateur world, but its place in our specialist age ought now to be questioned both as it affects individuals subjected to it, the class as a whole, and the quality and character of work produced.
>
> The man made to play cricket on Monday, rugger on Tuesday, snooker on Wednesday, badminton on Thursday, go swimming on Friday, tackle tiddlywinks on Saturday, and walk up a mountain on Sunday has no love for any of these activities—he merely flirts with them immorally. This in itself is unfortunate, but much more disturbing is the fact that this individual probably loses confidence and interest. Then he either retires behind a defensive barrier of cynical, if goodhumored, boredom and does not care whether he wins or loses, or else he develops an intense pathological determination not to be defeated or to unsportingly run the game. On the other hand, and this is an exceptionally important reflection, the first-class professional tennis player, recognized as an expert in one field, would probably disport himself with considerable aplomb and success when subjected to the melee of that week's activities; he will at least have some stroke play for cricket, speed for rugger, finesse for snooker, eye for badminton, muscle for swimming, cunning for tiddlywinks, and breath for mountaineering. Even more helpfully, he will have confidence justified by experience and success in one field and a balanced humility in not expecting prizes in the others, together with a humorous enthusiasm and interest in doing as well as he can within his self-acknowledged limitations.[6]

The notion that mobility *per se* is good stems in part from the desire to assure that all activities of the Executive Branch shall be integrated under, and responsive to, the leadership of the President. Yet, presidential leadership and effective program administration are not antithetical. The President can maintain his leadership over all Executive agencies and departments through the appointment of loyal heads of agencies and departments who bring to each organization the President's ideas and objectives, and through the effectiveness of his

---

[6] *The Economist*, August 8, 1964, p. 556.

control—through the Executive Office—of the budget and legislative proposals. It is the epitome of poor management to attempt (as some have suggested) to maintain a corps of interchangeable career administrators to be assigned to the individual agencies and departments as "his men." Such assignments would limit the effectiveness of the agency's or department's staff and undercut the responsibility of the political head he presumably holds accountable.

But as Senator John F. Kennedy declared, "This is no time for overspecialized public servants who are unable to ride easily over broad fields of knowledge."[7] To develop the broader kind of people he had in mind, it is necessary to provide a very carefully planned succession of assignments, under broad-gauged leaders, in a given program field; i.e., atomic energy, urban renewal, or the regulation of air transport. The intent would be to expand steadily the individual's understanding of his field and to develop the managerial skills he requires. At the same time, this would give him recognition in his chosen area and widen his acquaintanceship among those people in it "who count."[8]

Such carefully considered planning may require that the individual serve in the field as well as at headquarters, in a staff as well as in a line capacity, and in two or more agencies or departments. This also would include a stint as a staff assistant for a legislative committee or member—but only if such successive assignments are to provide a broadened understanding of a particular program field. The means by which an appropriate mix of assignments are defined and the adequacy of present definitions of "program fields" are subjects that well deserve additional research to provide improved bases for individual career planning.

Such considered planning of the individual's mobility can now be found in very few federal agencies and departments. What mobility does exist is usually the consequence of the in-

[7] Kennedy, *op. cit.*

[8] An excellent statement of the need and of the direction in which progress will be found was presented by Rufus E. Miles, Jr., *op. cit.*

dividual's own opportunistic shopping around during his early years in the service, and yields no combination of experience that significantly equips him for service at top levels.

c) *Developing by "Stepping Out"*

The development of the federal career servant will be best accomplished if, at one or more stages in his career, he is removed from the provincial influences of his agency or department and subjected to a broadening influence. Organizations vary markedly in the extent to which they encourage, accept, or will suffer constructive criticism of existing policies and practices. But every organization—private or public—demands of its members not only a familiarity with its policies but also a loyalty to them. This makes it desirable that those who will serve at the top be removed for a time from the constricting influence of the organization and made to view the organization and its program from without.

For most career men and women there is an urgent need, after six to eight years in the public service, for a rigorous stocktaking of what they have learned regarding the direction of their work and the function of other units of the agency and of the government. Simultaneously, this is the time for them to begin to underpin their personal philosophy of public service with clear thinking as to the role of government in relation to the individual, the society, and the economy.

If they are to be enabled to "dust off" the intellectual inventory they accumulate from experience, to classify this stock-on-hand that it may be readily available to them as a tool, they need an opportunity to step out of the federal agency and consider where they are and what they require to move ahead. They need a chance to examine critically the processes of the agency of which they are a part in a detached setting, unhampered by the parochial constraints that inevitably, and should, obtain within.

Later in the careers of the ablest career men and women, perhaps after twelve to twenty years of service, the problem of obsolescence occurs. For the program manager, the supporting staff manager, and the professional alike, there is need of replacing old knowledge and old skills with the new. The higher the career executive rises and the more years that elapse after he commences his career, the greater is his need for replacing the obsolescent both in his understanding of the substantive field and in administrative technique. The rapid advance in science and technology makes it essential that the scientific administrator periodically update what he knows of the field in which he once may have been a broadly and intensively equipped specialist. Similarly, the continual development of decision-making, planning, and control processes and the changes in the make-up of the workforce make necessary the substitution, for methods he learned by example, of advanced and previously unknown methods.

Consider but two illustrations: An outstanding physicist working in the space program, fifteen years after he received his Ph.D. and five years after he had been catapulted from the laboratory bench by advancement to an administrative position, seeks an opportunity to catch up, an opportunity to expand the understanding he brought with him from graduate school and the narrow additional understanding he has gained in a specialized program. Another career executive, who has presided for more than a decade over an agency with 35,000 employees, is confronted with a succession of proposals for the introduction of new programming, decision-making, and control techniques. He feels incapable of evaluating these proposals. Should he insist upon maintaining the "tried-and-true" processes with which he is familiar? Should he blindly accept his staff's proposals? Or should he find an opportunity to update his understanding in fields in which he feels less confident than he once did?

Both of these men, and many like them, require detachment and stimulation. William James once wrote of the infinite scarcity of individuals with "the capacity for nonhabitual perception," i.e., of looking at customary problems in uncustomary ways. Most men, as they grow older, find it more difficult to adopt new ways and to embrace new ideas. To refresh their spirits, to make more flexible their reasoning processes, as well as to acquaint themselves with the new that should replace the obsolete in what they earlier learned, they need detachment from the customary environment. The stimulation of new faces and new places can be provided in three ways.

1. *A first-rate university* can provide such stimulation, but only if it recognizes the individual's own need and does not force him into a rigid program reflecting the faculty's conception of a public executive's needs, or into courses and seminars designed for the training of Ph.D. candidates in teaching and research. The proposed "Federal Staff College," if it is adopted, must be so structured as to provide the detachment, stimulation, and individual opportunity or it will add little of consequence to the development of public executives.

2. *A foreign aid assignment* will provide for many both the detachment and the supplementary experience required. An assignment of three months to three years to another country, aiding it to develop governmental services under the aegis of our foreign aid program, may stimulate the individual to assess the policies and practices of his own agency more effectively than a like time at any university. But these assignments have seldom been made to broaden the competence and the viewpoint of the individual. There is much reason to believe that a planned program that would take at least 1,000 to 1,500 individuals occupying positions at grades GS-15 and above abroad each year on carefully articulated assignments would add materially to the vitality of the federal service, and at the same time it would contribute valuable assistance to the countries they would serve.

3. *An opportunity to work in a private business enterprise* will provide some individuals in some program fields the needed detachment, stimulation, and broadened perspective. This idea has been advanced by others in the past and their failure to effectuate such assignments testifies to the difficulties involved in creating such opportunities. Yet in a free-enterprise society, an expanding government with increasingly closer relations with the business community may well seek for its key career people this kind of experience.

Tenure for Those at the Top

Two aspects of the development of the American society bid
fair to modify existing policies as to the assurance of indefinite
tenure for all federal career servants. The first is the rapid
advance in the technology of the physical and social sciences
which tends to render obsolete more quickly the skills and
understandings of many who reach top-level positions. The
second is the existence of relatively full employment. In a
society characterized by effectively full employment, unemployment among highly educated and experienced individuals
is minimal, and hence, an original reason for the assurance of
indefinite tenure is reduced in force or no longer exists.

Simultaneously, the political heads of agencies and departments repeatedly find the need for replacing top-level career
people with others holding beliefs more nearly akin to their
own political views. The more dedication the individual
manifests to a program, the more often will a new political head
find it desirable to replace the individual when his dedication
smacks of an allegiance to the policies of the previous political
head.

These three factors—the advance in technology, the existence
of full employment, and the demand for politically responsive
individuals in top-level positions—make essential the recon-
sideration of existing tenure policies. So long as tenure is a
generally accepted element of compensation for the more
talented in the American society, the federal government will
have to provide the assurance of indefinite tenure for those
who choose a career in the federal service. That assurance
must not prevent more rapid turnover of those in the topmost
echelons than has prevailed in the past if the federal government is to maintain "capable managerial and professional
men and women in the topmost career posts in the Executive
Branch."

Two steps are needed. First, the establishment of a process
of "selection-out," i.e., a rigorous annual evaluation of all
individuals serving in the three topmost echelons of the federal

service and the elimination from the service of the one-fifth or one-eighth of those then serving who are no longer growing in their capacity to discharge highly important duties. Second, in order to maintain and improve the government's ability to recruit and retain men and women of the highest order of competence, the nature of the tenure now assured individuals should be modified. The kind of modification required has been effectively described by the Conference on the Public Service.

> When executives in good standing [We interpret this to mean individuals who survive the annual selection-out process referred to above.] are transferred or displaced at the convenience of the government, the government should either find the displaced officer another position of comparable rank and salary, or continue his former salary for a certain period of time in the most suitable job that can be found, regardless of its position classification. The latter privilege also should be available to executives who seek transfers. The government should also be willing to increase tangible benefits to some of its higher civil servants in order to attain this greater freedom of assignment. This might involve such things as higher salaries and guaranteeing fair market value on disposition of residence, when the individual is moved to a new job location, for example, from Washington to the field.[9]

In summary, there is need for abandoning the present concept of relating tenure to the particular job in which the individual currently serves, at least for those who are recruited for, or promoted to, positions in the three topmost echelons.

A SUMMARY OF WHAT NEEDS TO BE DONE

If the federal government is to maintain "capable managerial and professional staffs in the Executive Branch," the President and his principal aides, especially the Chairman of the United States Civil Service Commission and the Director of the Bureau of the Budget, must recurringly focus earnest attention on four

---

[9] Included in a letter by Roger Jones, Chairman, Conference on the Public Service, dated February 15, 1965, and addressed to Kermit Gordon, then director of the Bureau of the Budget, and John W. Macy, Jr., Chairman, United States Civil Service Commission.

aspects of the process by which men and women are brought into the positions at the three topmost echelons of the federal career service.

—*Recruitment.* Here there is a fourfold need for: (1) institutionalized foresight, i.e., periodically forecasting the number that will be required for each kind and occupational category of position that can be foreseen; (2) research that will show the way to ensuring that in the recruitment of able young college-trained people there is an adequate supply of talent that can be developed into broad-gauged top-level career servants for positions a score of years hence; (3) a more aggressive posture and increased efforts in competing for top talent to replenish the government's reservoir of promotable individuals; and (4) the encouragement of lateral entry of mature, experienced individuals from the outside directly into top-level positions.

—*Compensation.* Top-level career servants must be compensated at levels comparable to the compensation of men performing like work in private enterprise. This requires that ways be found and a rationale developed for measuring the compensation of individuals in private enterprise performing analogous work. The task calls for imagination—it is *not* (as technicians tend to protest) impossible. Also, the compensation of people serving in the three top echelons of the federal Executive Branch can and must be made to keep pace with rises in compensation in the private segment of the economy.

—*A More Considered Rationale of the Competences Required.* Most men and women who serve in top-level positions now have been developed within the federal service, and they will continue to be so. If they are to be equipped for the large responsibilities to be borne in top-level positions, a rationale must be developed to guide the actions that are taken in the name of development (i.e., supervision, reassignment and promotion, intra-agency and government-wide training). It is not enough to say that "broad visioned managers" are required; some more precise meaning must be given to such noble guides.

In summary, it is proposed that the vision must comprehend an intimate knowledge of the program the individual is associated with, of the internal and external environments with which he must cope, and of the processes of management, including particularly the arts of work direction and of communication. Finally, the competences required include a knowledge of how to apply these and related management arts in the particular program field or discipline in which the individual serves.

—A Policy of Career-Long Development. When a more considered rationale of the competences required by those who serve at the top is formulated, then there will remain need for regularly examining and improving the process of assignment and promotion, and the training that is now provided. All that is now done in these fields does not add up to an integrated effort to develop individuals in the light of a considered rationale as to the competences that are to be developed. It should. Hence, the need is for the establishment of a career-long process that will utilize all means (successive assignments, intra- and inter-agency training, and education at universities) to equip the individual with the variety of competences required at the top in the program field he has chosen.

APPENDIX A

THE PAY SCALES OF THE CLASSIFICATION ACT OF 1949, AS AMENDED BY THE FEDERAL EMPLOYEES SALARY ACT OF 1964

(The top line opposite each grade number shows the rates which became effective beginning with the first pay period on or after July 1, 1964. The second line shows the rates which were formerly in effect beginning with the first pay period on or after January 1, 1964.)

GENERAL SCHEDULE - BASIC PER ANNUM RATES

Grade	1	2	3	4	5	6	7	8	9	10	Amt. of Within-grade Increase
1	$3,385	$3,500	$3,615	$3,730	$3,845	$3,960	$4,075	$4,190	$4,305	$4,420	$115
	3,305	3,410	3,515	3,620	3,725	3,830	3,935	4,040	4,145	4,250	105
2	3,680	3,805	3,930	4,055	4,180	4,305	4,430	4,555	4,680	4,805	125
	3,620	3,725	3,830	3,935	4,040	4,145	4,250	4,355	4,460	4,565	105
3	4,005	4,140	4,275	4,410	4,545	4,680	4,815	4,950	5,085	5,220	135
	3,880	3,985	4,090	4,195	4,300	4,405	4,525	4,650	4,775	4,900	105–120 / 125
4	4,480	4,630	4,780	4,930	5,080	5,230	5,380	5,530	5,680	5,830	150
	4,215	4,335	4,495	4,635	4,775	4,915	5,055	5,195	5,335	5,475	140
5	5,000	5,165	5,330	5,495	5,660	5,825	5,990	6,155	6,320	6,485	165
	4,690	4,850	5,010	5,170	5,330	5,490	5,650	5,810	5,970	6,130	160
6	5,505	5,690	5,875	6,060	6,245	6,430	6,615	6,800	6,985	7,170	185
	5,235	5,410	5,585	5,760	5,935	6,110	6,285	6,460	6,635	6,810	175
7	6,050	6,250	6,450	6,650	6,850	7,050	7,250	7,450	7,650	7,850	200
	5,795	5,990	6,185	6,380	6,575	6,770	6,965	7,160	7,355	7,550	195
8	6,630	6,850	7,070	7,290	7,510	7,730	7,950	8,170	8,390	8,610	210
	6,390	6,600	6,810	7,020	7,230	7,440	7,650	7,860	8,070	8,280	210
9	7,220	7,465	7,710	7,955	8,200	8,445	8,690	8,935	9,180	9,425	245
	7,030	7,260	7,490	7,720	7,950	8,180	8,410	8,640	8,870	9,100	230
10	7,900	8,170	8,440	8,710	8,980	9,250	9,520	9,790	10,060	10,330	270
	7,690	7,945	8,200	8,455	8,710	8,965	9,220	9,475	9,730	9,985	255
11	8,650	8,945	9,240	9,535	9,830	10,125	10,420	10,715	11,010	11,305	295
	8,410	8,690	8,970	9,250	9,530	9,810	10,090	10,370	10,650		280
12	10,250	10,605	10,960	11,315	11,670	12,025	12,380	12,735	13,090	13,445	355
	9,980	10,310	10,640	10,970	11,300	11,63)	11,960	12,290	12,620		330
13	12,075	12,495	12,915	13,335	13,755	14,175	14,595	15,015	15,435	15,855	420
	11,725	12,110	12,495	12,880	13,265	13,650	14,035	14,420	14,805		385
14	14,170	14,660	15,150	15,640	16,130	16,620	17,110	17,600	18,090	18,580	490
	13,615	14,065	14,515	14,965	15,415	15,865	16,315	16,765	17,215		450
15	16,460	17,030	17,600	18,170	18,740	19,310	19,880	20,450	21,020	21,590	570
	15,665	16,180	16,695	17,210	17,725	18,240	18,755	19,270			515
16	18,935	19,590	20,245	20,900	21,555	22,210	22,865	23,520	24,175		655
	16,000	16,500	17,000	17,500	18,000						500
17	21,445	22,195	22,945	23,695	24,445						750
	18,000	18,500	19,000	19,500	20,000						500
18	24,500										
	20,000										

CSC FORM 2968
AUGUST 1964

CHARACTER OF THE GROUPS

CONCERNING THE WORK THEY DO

CAREER PATTERNS

Character of the Groups

Appendix Table 1.   Proportions in the Three Principal Groups

	Total number in group	Per cent
Program Managers	147	35
Supporting Staff Managers*	147	35
Professionals**	130	30
Total	424	100

* Includes 105 classified as Managerial Staff and 42 classified as Deputies or Assistants-to.
** Includes 86 classified as Professional Assistants and 44 classified as Performers.

Appendix Table 2. Average Age and Marital Status of Those in Each Group

	Average age*	Marital status			
		Married	Single	Widowed	Divorced
Program Managers . . .	53.6	138	4	3	2
Supporting Staff Managers	50.5	143	2	2	0
Professionals	51.9	127	1	2	0

* Average age for the entire sample is 52.0 years.

Appendix Table 3. Proportions in Three Principal Groups by Grade

	GS-16	GS-17	GS-18	PL-313 III	PL-313 II	PL-313 I
Program Managers . . .	77	33	15	5	8	9
Supporting Staff Managers	89	39	8	2	6	3
Professionals	51	16	2	15	29	17
Totals	217	88	25	22	43	29
Per cent	51	21	6	5	10	7

Appendix Table 4. Proportions in Three Principal Groups by Location

	Headquarters		Field	
Program Managers	120	81.6%	27	18.4%
Supporting Staff Managers	140	95.2	7	4.8
Professionals	93	72.0	37	28.0

Appendix Table 5. Education by Job Type*

Highest level of education attained	Program Managers	Supporting Staff Managers	Professionals
Less than high school graduate	1	0	0
High school graduate	5	2	1
College attended, but not graduate	10	17	0
College graduate	41	55	24
Master's degree	28	32	16
Ph.D.	22	14	50
LL.B.	27	24	27
M.D.	7	2	6
Other	6	0	6
Not reported	0	1	0
Totals	147	147	130

* Includes degrees attained *after* entry into federal service.

Appendix Table 6. Field of Study

Field	Program Managers	Supporting Staff Managers	Professionals
Accounting	10	13	2
Agricultural economics	4	0	1
Biology	1	1	4
Business administration	3	6	2
Economics	17	11	11
Education	1	6	0
English	0	2	1
Engineering: chemical, civil, electrical	9	12	14
Other engineering: architecture .	9	6	7
Forestry	3	0	0
Law	32	24	33
Medicine	7	2	6
Mathematics	0	2	3
Chemistry or physics	8	3	24
Physical science other than chemistry or physics	3	3	10
Public administration	3	9	1
Social science other than economics	9	6	4
Statistics	0	2	1
Other	12	19	5
No response	16	20	1
Totals	147	147	130

Concerning the Work They Do

Appendix Table 7. Average Number of Employees Supervised, by Location

	Headquarters	Field	For the total group
Program Managers	588	842	635
Supporting Staff Managers .	230	162	226
Professionals	100	213	132

Appendix Table 8. Average Number of Hours Worked for the Week Reported, by Location

	Headquarters	Field	For the total group
Program Managers	49.2	47.4	48.9
Supporting Staff Managers	49.0	44.4	48.7
Professionals	47.2	47.0	47.1

Appendix Table 9. Overtime Hours Worked, by Location*

	Headquarters	Field	For the total group
Program Managers	4.1	4.2	4.2
Supporting Staff Managers	3.1	2.9	3.1
Professionals	4.2	6.3	4.8

* Number of hours worked after 6:00 P.M. and on Saturday and Sunday.

Appendix Table 10. Does Respondent Work at Home in the Evening?

	Seldom	Often	Never	Total*
Program Managers	59	86	1	146
Supporting Staff Managers	55	89	1	145
Professionals	51	75	2	128
Totals	165	250	4	419
Per cent	39	59	1	99

* Of the 424 individuals who participated in this study, five (1 per cent) did not respond to this question.

Appendix Table 11. Average Hours Devoted to Specialized or Functional Activities, by Location*

	Headquarters	Field	For the total group
Program Managers	24.5	23.9	24.4
Supporting Staff Managers	26.3	24.7	26.2
Professionals	20.4	22.6	21.0

* Number of hours, during week reported on, devoted to meetings, discussions, phone calls, etc., where talking with others involved specialized or functional activities.

Appendix Table 12. Average Hours Devoted to General or Administrative Activities, by Location*

	Headquarters	Field	For the total group
Program Managers	4.0	4.7	4.1
Supporting Staff Managers	2.3	3.1	2.3
Professionals	2.3	4.4	2.9

* Number of hours, during week reported on, devoted to meetings, discussions, phone calls, etc., where talking with others involved general or administrative activities.

Appendix Table 13. Average Hours Spent Alone, by Location*

	Headquarters	Field	For the total group
Program Managers	13.4	13.1	13.4
Supporting Staff Managers	13.0	14.1	13.1
Professionals	18.3	15.5	17.5

* Number of hours during week reported on spent alone, reviewing mail, dictating, writing papers, reading, etc.

Career Patterns

Appendix Table 14. Length of Federal Service

Number of years	Program Managers	Supporting Staff Managers	Profes- sionals	Total for all groups	
Under 5	13	12	10	35	8.2%
5–9	5	9	8	22	5.2
10–14	17	13	16	46	10.9
15–19	13	25	29	67	15.8
20–24	27	39	34	100	23.6
25–29	43	29	21	93	21.9
30–34	14	17	6	37	8.7
35 and over	15	3	6	24	5.7
Totals	147	147	130	424	100.0%

Appendix Table 15. Age at Entry into Federal Service

Age ranges	Program Managers		Supporting Staff Managers		Professionals		Total for all groups	
Up to 20 . . .	9	6.1%	9	6.1%	4	3.1%	22	5.2%
21–25	49	33.3	48	32.7	28	21.5	125	29.5
26–30	29	19.7	37	25.2	39	30.0	105	24.8
31–40	44	30.0	36	24.5	44	33.8	124	29.2
41–50	10	6.8	14	9.5	12	9.2	36	8.5
51–60	5	3.4	3	2.0	1	0.8	9	2.1
Over 60 . . .	1	0.7	—	—	2	1.6	3	0.7
Totals . .	147	100.0%	147	100.0%	130	100.0%	424	100.0%

Appendix Table 16. Time of Entry into Federal Service

Entry period	Program Managers	Supporting Staff Managers	Professionals
Before 1933	29	15	10
1933–1940	65	54	43
1941–1945	16	30	32
1946–1952	19	30	27
1953–1960	8	9	13
1961 and after	10	9	5
Totals	147	147	130

Appendix Table 17. Starting Grade Level or Salary Group

Grade	Program Managers	Supporting Staff Managers	Profes-sionals	Total Number	Total Per cent
GS-1	6	14	1	21	5.0
GS-2	12	15	4	31	7.3
GS-3	6	7	6	19	4.5
GS-4	8	5	2	15	3.5
GS-5	33	22	24	79	18.6
GS-6	2	1	3	6	1.4
GS-7	21	18	22	61	14.4
GS-8	0	0	1	1	0.2
GS-9	10	10	11	31	7.3
GS-10	0	3	0	3	0.7
GS-11	15	11	17	43	10.1
GS-12	5	14	11	30	7.1
GS-13	6	5	6	17	4.0
GS-14	5	7	7	19	4.5
GS-15	5	7	6	18	4.3
GS-16	7	4	1	12	2.8
GS-17	1	0	1	2	0.5
GS-18	2	1	0	3	0.7
PL 313-III	3	0	3	6	1.4
PL 313-II	0	2	1	3	0.7
PL 313-I	0	1	3	4	1.0
Totals	147	147	130	424	100.0

Appendix Table 18. Average Number of Years of Service before Attaining Supergrade

Program Managers	17.8
Supporting Staff Managers	16.9
Professionals	15.4
Average for the total response	16.7

Appendix Table 19. Education at Entry into Federal Service

Level completed at entry	Program Managers		Supporting Staff Managers		Professionals	
High school	17	11.6%	22	15.0%	9	6.9%
College attended, but no degree	17	11.6	16	10.9	—	—
Bachelor's degree	66	44.9	72	49.0	60	46.2
Master's degree	24	16.2	24	16.3	16	12.3
Doctor's degree	23	15.7	13	8.8	45	34.6
Totals	147	100.0%	147	100.0%	130	100.0%

Appendix Table 20. Education: Was Highest Degree Attained after Entrance into Federal Service?

	Yes		No	
Program Managers	43	32.8%	88	67.2%
Supporting Staff Managers	37	29.1	90	70.9
Professionals	35	27.1	94	72.9
Totals*	115	29.7%	272	70.3%

* Of the 424 individuals who participated in this study, 37 (8.7 per cent) did not respond to this question.

Career Patterns

Appendix Table 21. Grade Levels Attained after Prescribed Periods of Service—Program Managers

Grade	Years of service completed						
	5	10	15	20	25	30	35
*	13	17	32	41	62	114	129
GS-1	0	0	0	0	0	0	0
GS-2	1	0	0	0	0	0	0
GS-3	3	0	0	0	0	0	0
GS-4	4	0	0	0	0	0	0
GS-5	10	3	1	0	0	0	0
GS-6	2	1	0	0	0	0	0
GS-7	14	10	2	1	0	0	0
GS-8	1	0	0	0	0	0	0
GS-9	20	7	1	1	0	0	0
GS-10	0	1	0	0	0	0	0
GS-11	23	24	10	1	1	0	0
GS-12	18	20	17	9	1	1	0
GS-13	18	21	17	7	8	3	1
GS-14	6	18	29	25	5	4	0
GS-15	6	17	26	32	30	5	5
GS-16	3	3	4	23	22	10	6
GS-17	1	1	4	3	12	4	3
GS-18	0	1	2	2	4	1	0
PL 313-III	2	1	1	1	2	2	1
PL 313-II	2	1	1	1	0	0	2
PL 313-I	0	1	0	0	0	3	0
	147	147	147	147	147	147	147

* No response: the respondent(s) has(have) not been in the federal service this long.

Appendix Table 22. Grade Levels Attained after Presecribed Periods of Service—Supporting Staff Managers

	Years of service completed						
Grade	5	10	15	20	25	30	35
*	11	17	31	52	89	124	142
GS-1	0	0	0	0	0	0	0
GS-2	0	0	0	0	0	0	0
GS-3	0	0	0	0	0	0	0
GS-4	7	0	0	0	0	0	0
GS-5	6	2	0	0	0	0	0
GS-6	3	0	0	0	0	0	0
GS-7	10	3	0	0	0	0	0
GS-8	2	1	0	0	0	0	0
GS-9	22	4	2	0	0	0	0
GS-10	2	1	0	0	0	0	0
GS-11	20	19	3	1	0	0	0
GS-12	15	22	12	3	1	0	0
GS-13	18	19	23	6	1	1	0
GS-14	10	22	21	17	4	1	1
GS-15	13	23	32	29	21	3	0
GS-16	6	10	14	30	25	15	3
GS-17	2	4	6	5	3	2	1
GS-18	0	0	1	1	1	1	0
PL 313-III	0	0	2	2	1	0	0
PL 313-II	0	0	0	0	1	0	0
PL 313-I	0	0	0	1	0	0	0
	147	147	147	147	147	147	147

* No response: the respondent(s) has (have) not been in the federal service this long.

Appendix Table 23. Grade Levels Attained after Prescribed Periods of Service—Professionals

Grade	Years of service completed						
	5	10	15	20	25	30	35
*	11	18	30	51	93	115	124
GS-1	0	0	0	0	0	0	0
GS-2	0	0	0	0	0	0	0
GS-3	0	0	0	0	0	0	0
GS-4	3	0	0	0	0	0	0
GS-5	3	2	0	0	0	0	0
GS-6	2	0	0	0	0	0	0
GS-7	7	2	1	0	0	0	0
GS-8	0	1	0	0	0	0	0
GS-9	14	3	1	0	0	0	0
GS-10	0	0	0	0	0	0	0
GS-11	19	10	3	1	0	0	0
GS-12	23	15	4	4	1	0	0
GS-13	16	24	12	2	2	1	0
GS-14	15	22	22	10	4	2	0
GS-15	7	19	26	22	8	2	2
GS-16	0	4	14	19	15	7	2
GS-17	1	0	0	4	0	2	1
GS-18	0	0	0	0	1	0	0
PL 313-III	4	6	10	12	2	0	1
PL 313-II	4	3	7	5	3	1	0
PL 313-I	1	1	0	0	1	0	0
	130	130	130	130	130	130	130

* No response: the respondent(s) has(have) not been in the federal service this long.

Appendix Table 24. Organizational Mobility: Number of Different Bureaus Worked In

	Number of bureaus					
	1	2	3	4	More than 4	Totals
Program Managers	67	39	24	15	2	147
Supporting Staff Managers	38	37	38	16	18	147
Professionals	61	40	14	12	3	130
Totals	166	116	76	43	23	424
Per cent	39.2	27.4	17.9	10.1	5.4	100

Appendix Table 25. Organizational Mobility: Are Respondents
Now Working in the Same Agencies or Departments
Their Federal Careers Started in?

	Yes	No	Total
Program Managers	83	64	147
Supporting Staff Managers	46	101	147
Professionals	72	58	130
Totals	201	223	424
Per cent	47.4	52.6	100

Appendix Table 26. Organizational Mobility: Have Respondents Worked
Outside of the Federal Service since Their Dates of Entry?

	Yes	No	Total
Program Managers	24	123	147
Supporting Staff Managers	19	128	147
Professionals	20	110	130
Totals	63	361	424
Per cent	14.9	85.1	100

Appendix Table 27. Occupational Mobility: Have All Jobs since Entry
into Federal Service Been in Same Occupational Group?

	Yes		No	
Program Managers	108	77.1%	32	22.9%
Supporting Staff Managers	101	71.1	41	28.9
Professionals	101	80.8	24	19.2
Totals*	310	76.2%	97	23.8%

* Of the 424 individuals who participated in the study, 17 (4 per cent) did not respond
to this question.

APPENDIX C

A STUDY OF THE ROLE PERFORMED
BY THE FEDERAL EXECUTIVE

PRINCETON UNIVERSITY — WITH THE ASSISTANCE OF McKINSEY & COMPANY, INC.

This questionnaire is a request for your assistance in a confidential study of *what* top-level Federal career executives do, *how* and *on what* they spend their time. Other studies have been concerned with who these executives are, where they come from, how rapidly they reached and how they were appointed to their present positions. This study is designed to reveal *what* they do, what role they perform.

To repeat, we seek your personal cooperation in supplying information that will shed light on the role performed by an increasingly important group of individuals in the American society. The results, we believe, will be helpful in creating greater appreciation of the contribution of the Federal career executive. A report of such conclusions as are developed will be sent to you when available in early 1964.

PART I — IDENTIFYING THE EXECUTIVE

Name: _____ _____ _____
             First   Middle   Last

Title of Position:_____

Department:_____ Bureau or Office:_____

Division:_____ Office Phone No.:_____ Ext._____

Number of employees for whom you

have overall responsibility:_____ Your Date of Birth:_____

Your Education: (*Circle correct answers*)   Your Marital Status: (*Check one*)

High School: College: Graduate School: Married_____ Widowed_____

                                               Single_____   Divorced_____
Attended   Attended   Attended
                                               Your Children:
Graduated   Graduated   Graduated
                                               Number:_____ Range in Age:_____

State degrees obtained, year each obtained, and major subject matter field

Degree	Year	Subject Matter Field

Job titles and classification sheets do not always reveal the real nature of a job. Please describe very briefly (three or four sentences) the nature of the job in which you now serve. Just picture, in words you might use in telling a new acquaintance what you do, what the job is all about.

_____

_____

_____

_____

177

PART II — CATEGORIZING YOUR CAREER PROGRESS

The purpose of the following questions is to obtain data which when correlated with data derived from Part III will provide an answer to this question: *Do men who have advanced by one career route (e.g., as a scientist, as a line operator, as personnel, budget, training or other staff man) use their time differently, when they have reached the top levels than those who have risen via another career route?*

When did you first enter the Federal service?_____ In what job? *(Give title and grade)*_____
                                       Year

Briefly describe type of work:_____

    Department:_____ Bureau or Organization:_____ Division:_____

For each succeeding job, please supply the following data. Please do not list jobs which, while different in title, grade, or salary, did not differ significantly from preceding ones in duties performed, or temporary jobs, or jobs in which you served less than six months. If at any time, since entry into the Federal service, you were employed outside the Federal government, please include and treat as other jobs except indicate in column headed "Department or Bureau" the nature of the employer, (e.g., "*private business*", "*state government*", etc.). Please use an additional sheet if the spaces provided below are not adequate.

Title of Job — Grade	Year Appointed	Department or Bureau	General Field of Work	At Headquarters or in Field
1.				
2.				
3.				
4.				
5.				

As you look back over the jobs listed above:
  (a) Was each in the same occupational group in which you are now working? Yes:____

    No:____; if answer is No, indicate which jobs were not in this occupational field:

_____

_____

_____

  (b) Did each contribute to your advancement to your present position? Yes:_____

    No:_____; if answer is No, which jobs did not contribute to your advancement

    and why:_____

_____

_____

In which of the following occupational groups would you say you are now working:

Social Science, Psychology and Welfare Group	_____	Miscellaneous Occupations Group	_____
General Administrative	_____	Personnel Administration and Industrial Relations Group	_____
Accounting and Budget Group	_____	Biological Sciences Group	_____
Veterinary Medical Science Group	_____	Medical, Hospital, Dental and Public Health Group	_____
Legal and Kindred Group	_____	Engineering and Architecture Group	_____
Business and Industry Group	_____	Information and Arts Group	_____
Physical Sciences Group	_____	Copyright, Patent and Trademark Group	_____
Mathematics and Statistics Group	_____	Library and Archives Group	_____
Education Group	_____	Investigation Group	_____
Supply Group	_____	Transportation Group	_____

PART III — ANALYZING THE USE OF YOUR TIME

Our hypothesis is that by learning how an executive uses his time, we can learn much about the role he plays. To learn how you use your time, we ask in subsequent pages that:

    A.   Your secretary record for the week after receipt of this questionnaire, as fully and revealingly as space and her time will permit, what you did with your time day by day.

    B.   You describe briefly illustrative activities that have consumed your time during the week for which the record is kept.

    C.   You respond to a series of questions in Part V that will help us interpret the data presented in Parts III and IV.

A NOTE TO YOUR SECRETARY AS TO HOW TO RECORD THE UTILIZATION OF TIME ON THE FOLLOWING ANALYSIS SHEET

The central purpose of this study is to determine *what the executive does with his time.* Hence, it will be especially helpful if in recording where the executive's time went, you will strive to indicate, as succinctly as possible, (a) *the substance of the matter* on which time was spent, *e.g.,* Reviewed draft testimony for Secretary to present to Congressional Committee on Small Business, Approved personnel promotions recommended by staff; (b) *what* was done about it — talked, read, dictated, telephoned, wrote; (c) *with whom* the talking or writing was done, *e.g.,* "telephoned opposite number in State Dept. re. . . . "; (d) *where* the activity took place — in executive's office, in other person's office, in a departmental conference room, in a Congressional committee room, or "at BOB".

We realize that the executive's time cannot be recorded precisely. It will not likely be possible to record what was done in each fifteen minutes throughout the day. Just estimate as closely as practicable how much time went into each meeting, each conference, the dictation of a report, reading and referring mail, etc. Mark the analysis sheet accordingly, *i.e.,* just draw a line across the daily column at the time an activity started and a second line when it stopped.

LUNCHEON, DINNER OR WEEKEND PERIODS. When the executive devoted his luncheon (or other "non-office hours") to official business, record this time just as you would other time spent on official business. Draw horizontal lines across the daily column when he went to lunch and when he returned and write in the substance of the matter covered and other information requested above. If his luncheon time was *not* devoted to official business, draw the horizontal lines to indicate time taken and write in "Lunch".

One final note: Please tally the number of incoming telephone calls he takes and the number of outgoing calls he makes. Space is provided on the analysis sheet for approximating the number of in and out calls.

ANALYSIS SHEET TO RECORD TIME UTILIZATION

This sheet is intended to aid your secretary in recording where your time went during the week under study, and to facilitate your answering the questions that follow. We attach an extra copy that your secretary may use as a work sheet as the week progresses. Space (and the time of your secretary) is limited, but *the fuller and the more descriptive the statements included can be made, the more useful this record will be.* Please add additional sheets if necessary. Thank you.

Name_____

Week ending_____1963.

Starting Time (State Hour)	Monday	Tuesday	Wednesday	Thursday	Friday	Saturday	Sunday
8:00- 8:15 am 8:15- 8:30 8:30- 8:45 8:45- 9:00 9:00- 9:15 9:15- 9:30 9:30- 9:45 9:45-10:00							
10:00-10:15 am 10:15-10:30 10:30-10:45 10:45-11:00 11:00-11:15 11:15-11:30 11:30-11:45 11:45-12:00							
12:00-12:15 pm 12:15-12:30 12:30-12:45 12:45- 1:00 1:00- 1:15 1:15- 1:30 1:30- 1:45 1:45- 2:00							
2:00- 2:15 pm 2:15- 2:30 2:30- 2:45 2:45- 3:00 3:00- 3:15 3:15- 3:30 3:30- 3:45 3:45- 4:00							
4:00- 4:15 pm 4:15- 4:30 4:30- 4:45 4:45- 5:00 5:00- 5:15 5:15- 5:30 5:30- 5:45 5:45- 6:00-							
After 6:00 p.m.							
Total Hours							
Approximate Number of Telephone Calls Incoming							
Outgoing							

PART IV — ILLUSTRATING THE USE OF YOUR TIME

Do you have *substantial* command over how your time is distributed among the activities

recorded on the preceding analysis sheet? Yes_____ No_____ ;

if answer is No, please state briefly why._____

_____

_____

A — As you look back over the record of a week's activities, what were the *more significant* activities? More specifically, in the space below, please describe briefly those projects, meetings, reports, memoranda, conferences (with superiors, with your own staff, or with representatives of other departments, or members of Congress) that were relatively of greater significance.

Don't be misled by your familiarity with the tasks you work on to conclude that few or none of your activities were *"more significant."* Please describe 4 or 5 or more activities that, relative to other activities involved in your job, were the *"more significant,"* and indicate briefly why the activity was significant.

For each activity cited in response to this and the following question, please state:

- (a) *The objective or substance of the activity, e.g.,* the development of a budget, the preparation of a report on _____ , the conduct of a laboratory experiment, the drafting of a speech, the recommendation of an individual for appointment, or the persuasion of the individual to accept appointment, etc.
- (b) *The nature of the activity, i.e.,* what was done about it — talk, confer, dictate, read, write.
- (c) *With whom* the talking, conferring, or telephoning was done — your superiors; your subordinates; immediate personal staffs; your peers, others in the department of like rank or professional colleagues; congressmen, their staffs, or committee staffs; representatives of constituencies (*e.g.,* the AFL-CIO or the American Legion); members of the general public; representatives of the press, radio or TV; others.
- (d) *Who initiated* the activity — you did; your staff did; your superior(s) did; one of your peers; or others listed in (c).
- (e) *Where* the activity took place — in your office; in a subordinate's office; in a peer's office; in a conference room of your department or agency; in the offices of another department or agency; in the offices or committee rooms of Congress; in public buildings (*e.g.,* a hotel for lunch or a convention hall for a speech); out of town when in travel status; other.
- (f) *How much time was taken* — please approximate the time (*e.g.,* to the quarter hour, "1¼ hours") that was taken in disposing of this particular activity.

1. _____

_____

_____

2. _____

_____

_____

3. _____

_____

_____

4. _____

_____

_____

5. _____

_____

_____

B — As you look back over the record of a week's activities what were the *least significant* activities that took your time? Stated in other words, what 4 or 5 or more relatively routine or unimportant meetings, conferences with other officials of the department or of other departments, what reports, memoranda or other activities took your time?

Please describe, in the space below, with respect to each such activity — its substance, *what* was done, *with whom*, *who* initiated the activity, or *what* requirement necessitated that you spent time on this activity, *why* you regard the activity as relatively least significant, and approximately how much time it took.

1. _____

_____

_____

2. _____

_____

_____

3. _____

_____

_____

4. _____

_____

_____

5. _____

_____

_____

PART V — INTERPRETING THE ANALYSIS OF YOUR TIME

A — Can you approximate, for the past week, what *proportion* of the total time you devoted to the job (during and after working hours) was taken by each of the following functions, and will you *illustrate* the kind of activity you classify under each functional heading by referring to activities cited in Part IV; *e.g.,* Item 2 in Part IV (A or B) *A,* on page 6. Functions that cannot be related to items in Part IV may be illustrated by other activities on an additional sheet.

Before approximating the proportion of your time that went into each of several functions, please answer these questions:

    1. At what time do you usually start work in the morning? _____a.m.
    2. At what time do you usually leave for home in the evening? _____ p.m.

3. Do you work at home in the evening? (*Circle the correct answer*) Seldom Often Never
4. Approximately how many hours did you work during the past week on matters of official business? _____ hours

Then read definitions of each function stated in the box at the bottom of this page and answer these queries:

Performing: Approximate proportion of total time devoted to activities classified under this function _____ % Illustration: Item_____, Part IV_____, page_____

Planning: Approximate proportion of total time devoted to activities classified under this function _____ % Illustration: Item_____, Part IV_____, page_____

Controlling: Approximate proportion of total time devoted to activities classified under this function _____ % Illustration: Item_____, Part IV_____, page_____

Coordinating: Approximate proportion of total time devoted to activities classified under this function _____ % Illustration: Item_____, Part IV_____, page_____

Evaluating: Approximate proportion of total time devoted to activities classified under this function _____ % Illustration: Item_____, Part IV_____, page_____

Negotiating: Approximate proportion of total time devoted to activities classified under this function _____ % Illustration: Item_____, Part IV_____, page_____

Representing: Approximate proportion of total time devoted to activities classified under this function _____ % Illustration: Item_____, Part IV_____, page_____

Staffing: Approximate proportion of total time devoted to activities classified under this function _____ % Illustration: Item_____, Part IV_____, page_____

Supervising: Approximate proportion of total time devoted to activities classified under this function _____ % Illustration: Item_____, Part IV_____, page_____

Supplying: Approximate proportion of total time devoted to activities classified under this function _____ % Illustration: Item_____, Part IV_____, page_____

_____: Approximate proportion of total time devoted to activities classified under this function _____ % Illustration: Item_____, Part IV_____, page_____

DEFINITIONS OF FUNCTIONS

PROGRAM FUNCTIONS:

Performing: This term is used to describe those activities you engage in in which you further the work of your organization *directly* rather than indirectly through others. The personal preparation of a report, a substantive memorandum, or the personal drafting of legislation. Or for the scientist, under this code should be recorded that time that you devote to research, to the preparation of a report or a scientific paper.

Planning: Determining goals, policies and courses of action. Work scheduling for whole staff or major units, budgeting, setting up procedures, establishing goals or standards, preparing agendas, programming.

Controlling: This is the function of "keeping on top of the job"; it comprehends the collecting and analyzing of information as to how the total operation or major segments of it are going. It involves the study of records, reports and accounts; inventorying, measuring output, preparing summary reports for superiors and inspecting operations in the offices of subordinates or in field offices.

Coordinating: Exchanging information with people in the organization other than your subordinates (record time devoted to the exchange of information with your subordinates under "Supervising") in order to relate and adjust programs. Advising other departments, expediting, liaison with other officials, arranging meetings, informing superiors, seeking other bureaus' and other departments' cooperation.

Evaluating: Assessing and appraising proposals and reported or observed performance. Appraising individual and group employee performance, judging the quality and output of product, judging financial reports, inspecting operations, and evaluating proposals and suggestions.

Negotiating: Dealing with review and control agencies within the Department (*e.g.,* Administrative Assistant Secretary's staff), within the Executive Branch (*e.g.,* U.S. Civil Service Commission), and with committees of Congress on program matters.

Representing: Advancing the general interests of your bureau or department through speeches, consultation and contacts with individuals, groups or constituencies outside the organization. Public speeches, meetings with professional groups (*e.g.,* the AF of L), community drives, news releases, and conventions and conferences.

ADMINISTRATIVE FUNCTIONS:

Staffing: Maintaining and building the effectiveness of your staff. Recruiting new staff members, interviewing prospective staff members, selecting employees, placing employees, promoting employees, transferring employees.

Supervising: Directing, leading and reviewing the work of subordinates. Counseling subordinates, training subordinates as individuals, explaining assignments and work rules, disciplining and handling of complaints.

Supplying: Planning for and obtaining the space, equipment, supplies and other nonfinancial resources required for accomplishment of the work of the bureau. division or office you head.

B — Is the week for which these proportions and illustrations are given typical in respect to the use of your time? (*Circle the correct answer*)   Yes   No
Why or why not?_____

_____

_____

_____

C — Are there activities which constitute an integral part of your job which did *not* claim a portion of your time during the week for which a record was kept? For example, representing your bureau or department before the Bureau of the Budget, before Congressional committees, or negotiating with constituent groups (*e.g.*, Aerospace Industries Association), or speaking before civic groups. Please indicate what *you* do with respect to each such activity and approximate the man-days devoted to such activity over the past twelve months._____

D — A final question. What kinds of experience and education in what fields would you prescribe for the man who might succeed you in this job if you were to leave next week? Why?_____

Note: *If you believe that the answers to this questionnaire do not fully depict the nature of your activities or the utilization of your time please add such comments or opinions as will help us understand more accurately the role you perform as a Federal executive.*

PLEASE RETURN TO: **JOHN J. CORSON
SUITE 509
1625 EYE STREET, N.W.
WASHINGTON 6, D.C.**

INDEX

Acheson, Dean, 31
Ades, Dr. Harlow W., 79
Administrative Conference of the United States, 30
Advanced Research Projects Agency, 85
Advisory Commission on Intergovernmental Relations, 59
Aerospace Industries Association, 69
Agency for International Development (AID), 5, 6–7, 26, 33, 50, 55
Air Force Association, 69
Air Transport Association, 95n
American Association of Railroads, 96
American Bar Association, 29–30
American Cancer Society, 95n
American Federation of Labor–Congress of Industrial Organizations (AFL-CIO), 30, 40
American Legion, 40
American Medical Association, 95n
American Mining Congress, 95n
American Municipal Association, 59
American Society for Public Administration, 61n, 75n, 102n, 134n
American Telephone and Telegraph Company, 136n, 137
Armed Services Technical Information Agency, 42
Atomic Energy Commission (AEC), 5, 16n, 77n, 95n, 127

Bacon, Donald W., 52
Bakke, Wight, 146
Ball, Robert, 39n
Barzun, Jacques, 149
Bennett, James V., 39n
Bluestone, Dr. David W., 80
British Civil Service, 153
British Defense Department, 93
Brown, Dr. David S., 56n
Browning, Joe L., 23, 25, 132

Bureau of the Budget, 7, 28, 34, 36, 38, 59, 66, 69, 73, 74, 75, 120–21, 159
Bureau of Mines, 95n
Bureau of Prisons, 39n, 42
Bureau of Public Roads, 59, 148
Bureau of Standards, 77n, 95n

Call, Cornelius K., 24, 25
Cape Kennedy, 60
Carlson, S., 14n
Carroll, S. J., 11n
Castro, Fidel, 57
Central Intelligence Agency (CIA), 70, 100n
Chermak, Dr. Lawrence E., 81
Civil Aeronautics Authority (CAA), 61
Civil Aeronautics Board (CAB), 24, 32, 69, 80, 121, 136
Civil Service Commission, United States: 2, 7, 13, 32, 62, 69–70, 75, 123, 159; functions, 74; and *Quality Graduate Program*, 111n. See also British Civil Service; New York State Civil Service
Claxton, P. P., 68n
Coast and Geodetic Survey (C&GS), 77n, 86
Collins, O. F., 3n See also Warner, W. L.
Columbia University, 136n, 139n
Committee for Economic Development (CED), 125n
Conference on the Public Service, 159
Congress: and Military Assistance Program, 8; and professionals, 91, 95, 96–7, 101; and program manager, 21, 23, 29, 30, 34, 35, 37, 38–9, 42–3, 47, 50, 104; and supporting staff manager, 53, 54–5, 65–8, 70, 71, 73
Congressional committees. See House; Senate.
Cornell University, 51
Corson, John J., 134n, 141n

Halle, Louis J., 31*n*
Haskell, Dr. Norman A., 80
Herma, J. L., 139*n*
Home Loan Bank Board, 129
Hoover Commission, 39*n*
Hoover, J. Edgar, 49
House and Senate Agriculture and
 Public Works Committees, 35
House and Senate Banking Committees,
 96
House Appropriations Subcommittee,
 35, 38, 69, 75, 97. *See also* Senate
 House Ways and Means Committee, 38
Housing and Home Finance Agency
 (HHFA), 58, 60
Hume, Gray W., 53

*Improving Executive Management in the
 Federal Government*, 125*n*
Internal Revenue Service (IRS): 11, 25,
 29, 32, 40, 55, 57, 71, 80, 88, 129, 133;
 and community support, 147; and political appointees,127;and professionals,
 92, 101; structure, 52–4
Interstate Commerce Commission (ICC),
 34

James, William, 156
Jennings, M. K., 3*n*. *See also* Kilpatrick,
 F. P.
Jerdee, T. H., 11*n*
Jewish War Veterans, 40
Johnson, Lyndon B., 68
Joint Chiefs of Staff, 8
Jones, Roger, 159*n*

Kappel, Frederick R., 136*n*
Kennedy Administration, 31
Kennedy, John F., 31, 100*n*, 108, 149*n*,
 154
Kilpatrick, F. P., 3*n*, 12, 13*n*, 108*n*

Leffingwell, William M., 7–9
Lend-Lease, 9
Likert, Rensis, 146*n*
Litchfield, Edward H., 12*n*
Lubin, Isador, 39*n*

McCleery, William, 51*n*
McCrensky, Edward, 115
McHugh, John L., 60
McIntyre, Robert V., 24, 25
McKinsey and Company, 141*n*, 177
MacMahon, A., 1*n*
McNair, Bruce, 53

Macy, John W., Jr., 159*n*
Mahoney, T. A., 11*n*
Management: as a group process, 49–50;
 and communication, 50–1; and correla-
 tion, 47–8; definition of, 12; functions,
 150*n*; in federal government, 1, 13,
 22–3, 44; and innovation, 46–7;
 internal, 10; leadership, 33–4; loose-
 ness of term, 11, 12; and negotiation,
 48–9; and program, 44–6; skills of, 43
Mandell, M. M., 14*n*
Mannes, Marya, 48
Maritime Administration, 27
Martin, N. H., 3*n*. *See also* Warner, W. L.
Medicare, 9, 83
Meredith College, 10
Meriam, Lewis, 128*n*
Miles, Rufus E., Jr., 117, 128, 154*n*
Military Assistance Program, 7–8
Millett, J., 1*n*
Museum of Natural History, 120
Myers, Robert J., 83

National Academy of Sciences, 95*n*
National Aeronautics and Space Ad-
 ministration (NASA), 17, 77*n*, 79,
 95*n*, 101, 140*n*, 151
National Association of Manufacturers
 (NAM), 30
National Bureau of Standards, 77*n*, 89,
 95*n*
National Conference on Social Welfare,
 10
National Housing Agency, 119
National Institute of Mental Health
 (NIMH), 39*n*, 83–4
National Oceanographic program, 60*n*
National Park Service, 4, 36, 37, 61
National Resources Planning Board, 10
National Security Industrial Association,
 69
National Wheat Growers Association, 96
New York State Civil Service, 141*n*

Patent Examining Corps, 29
Perkins, James A., 51
Pfiffner, John, 72
Political appointees, 4, 5, 6, 24, 25, 34,
 46, 49, 51, 127
Pollock, R., 16*n*, 78*n*
Postal Field Service, 5
Post Office Department, 64*n*, 73, 96, 119
Preston, Edward F., 53
Princeton University, 115*n*, 177
Professionals: age, 82, 110, 165, 170;

MEN NEAR THE TOP

Filling Key Posts in the Federal Service

By John J. Corson and R. Shale Paul

designer: Edward King
typesetter: Baltimore Type and Composition Corporation
typefaces: Baskerville Display and Text
printer: The Murray Printing Company
paper: Perkins and Squier Glatfelter Offset
binder: The Murray Printing Co. and William Marley Company
cover material: Bancroft Arestox Linen Finish